LINGUISTICS, LANGUAGE
AND RELIGION

IS VOLUME

126

OF THE

Twentieth Century Encyclopedia of Catholicism

UNDER SECTION

XIII

CATHOLICISM AND SCIENCE

IT IS ALSO THE

129TH

VOLUME IN ORDER OF PUBLICATION

Edited by **HENRI DANIEL-ROPS** *of the Académie Française*

LINGUISTICS, LANGUAGE AND RELIGION

By DAVID CRYSTAL

HAWTHORN BOOKS · PUBLISHERS · *New York*

First Edition, April, 1965

NIHIL OBSTAT

Joannes M. T. Barton, S.T.D., L.S.S.

Censor Deputatus

IMPRIMATUR

Patritius Casey

Vicarius Generalis

Westmonasterii, die II FEBRUARII MCMLXV

H-9556

CONTENTS

INTRODUCTION

The Oxford English Dictionary soberly informs us that the word "linguistics" first appears in English in 1855; yet despite a century of scientifically-stimulated growth, the word, if injected into a non-specialist discussion, still produces more incomprehension and uninformed generalization than anything else. Linguistics has something to do with language, but exactly what, few people seem to know. To the majority, a linguist is a familiar personality: he is a man who speaks many languages, who perhaps works for a foreign office or a tourist agency. But about language itself, there is less agreement: on the one hand, it is seen as "something which happens", that can be taken for granted or completely ignored; on the other hand, it is something one complains vociferously about to the local Press or takes stumbling steps to acquire at holiday-time. To a few, its importance is appreciated as an essential aspect of day-to-day existence, as a part of living, or of earning a living, or simply as a fascinating object of study. Language can be magical, mysterious, emotionful; or it can be impersonal, utilitarian, a tool. But it is above all a fact; and man, being a kind of social animal, uses this complex, many-sided fact nine-tenths of the time he ever devotes to communication, which is the hallmark of his sociability.

It would seem, then, to be a highly important fact, particularly these days, when the need for better international and intranational communication is being emphasized. Language *qua* potential communication barrier has made more people than ever look upon it with new interest, as "the learnable aspect of other people's behaviour", which was how the anthropologist Margaret Mead put it. But, as the language-users are beginning to discover, there are many kinds of barrier, of which a foreign language is just one example: far more effective is the barrier of a common language. And any study which claims to be a science of language, a linguistics, must then be prepared to deal with much more than problems of translation at Calais or Caernarvon. Language has a multiplicity of purposes, a multitude of social functions, and linguistics studies them all. But in particular, linguistics studies language phenomena as an end in itself, as an aspect of human behaviour which no other animal possesses. It is thus primarily a "pure" discipline, only secondarily a social service, though the range of applications is vast, and relevant to all cultures, be they humanities, sciences, or in between.

Religion is one such field which could well use the information about language that linguistics can provide—information about terminology, definition, ambiguity, vernacular, techniques of communication, for example—but the recent Vatican Council is perhaps the only major sign this century that it is prepared to do so. There are two positions involved, which are inherent in the relationship existing between religion and any sphere of scientific progress: a defensive and a constructive. The former is required when scientific or intellectual developments are utilized by opponents of religion to the detriment of the Church and its teaching—when the study of language, for example, provided a flame for what came to be known as logical positivism. The latter is more pervasive and more important: it attempts to appreciate and assimilate what the new study has to offer, so that the traditional message can be presented in an up-to-date way and shown to be compatible with the results of such research. In a book on language and religion, orientation is specific, for in the final analysis, all that the Church is trying to do is tell a world about a Man and what he stood for—trying to communicate, in words, what he, using words, told it. The relevance of the science which studies language is clear. If you want to convert the man in the street, then you need to speak *his* language (because he feels no need of yours), and this means knowing what his language is, and how and why it differs from yours. Carelessness in communication is fatal in any business, eternal or otherwise. You do not call your neighbour "perfidious" if you want him to sympathize with you; nor do you stay patient with a jargon that may satisfy you, but which he cannot comprehend.

A linguist—or, as some now say, a linguistician—is one who provides a point of view and a technique for talking *about* language, so that man can know more about it, his unique attribute. To do this, he needs to amass a great deal of information about the world's languages and the way individuals treat their language. Then, but only then, the results of his researches can be channelled into other areas where they can be of use —this is applied linguistics. At the time of writing, the fruitful nature of these occupations is evidenced by many bulky bibliographies, but they largely cater for the specialist. The linguistic renaissance which has taken place this century has reverberated little beyond the Universities. There is no up-to-date guide to the subject for the non-specialist; which is a gross lack of understanding on the part of the academic linguistician, because he is failing to satisfy a natural curiosity in the phenomenon of language that has never waned among human beings, and which has been more recently set on edge by the regular murmurs in the Press and on television. This little book can only begin to survey the multi-branching discipline. It aims to provide some idea of what is involved in studying language. It must be brief, and simplification can only be alleviated by the footnote references, of which there are many, so that the interested reader can be his own pioneer elsewhere. Above all, the book makes little claim to be original; the attempt is critically to survey the ground rather than add to it. Nevertheless, the novelty of the discipline's ideas to many, it is hoped, will stimulate further thought on some important issues.

The first chapters, then, describe something of the background to modern linguistics, and introduce some general ideas; Chapters V–VIII go on to cover the many pure and applied aspects of the contemporary scene; Chapters IX–XII then discuss some of the specifically religious implications that arise

from study of the subject. As J. R. Firth said, at the very beginning of his *Tongues of Man* (London, 1937): "the notions men
have about language derive from their particular type of society
and cultural inheritance, and especially from their religion." It
will be seen that religion can learn much more from the scientific study of language than language ever learned from it.

CHAPTER I

THE CLASSICAL POINTS
OF VIEW

I do believe,
Though I have found them not, that there may be
Words which are things.
(Byron, *Childe Harold*.)

As was pointed out in the Introduction, man has never ceased
to worry over or be curious about his language. The columns of
writing, from Herodotus to the *Radio Times*, display him both
as logophobe and logophile. What justifies the term "renaissance" in describing twentieth-century views on language, then,
is the novelty of a more scientific approach to the subject. The
study of language has been put in a new perspective over the
last fifty years; it has become an autonomous discipline, and
now scholars are trained and paid to continue the study. The
professional status is something quite different from the past,
when language studies were always subservient to the requirements of logic, rhetoric, philosophy, history or literary criticism.
But it took over a century of methodical research to bring such
respect and independence. And since the early 1800's, there has
been a newfound and meticulous empiricism, a desire to clarify
terminology and to formalize basic assumptions and principles,
and a cementing in the overall framework of cultural anthropology, all of which has produced this new orientation that can
genuinely be called a renaissance.

But this brave New World cannot be understood without
some knowledge of the Old. The history of linguistics is filled

with random, amateur observations, mainly to do with the origins and nature of language, speech and writing, which need to be at least briefly surveyed before discussing the modern state of the subject which we call linguistics. Western civilization, and Christianity in particular, is indeed well documented with background material of this kind, since more written records have survived. And such records shed an interesting light on modern problems, attitudes and ideas, for the focus of attention is the same now, as then; they can only help to increase our appreciation of the subject.

THE GREEKS

For the most part, these records, covering a period of over two thousand years, deal with only two themes: where did language come from, and, now we have it, what is the relationship between words and things? In some writers the problems were inseparable; others record isolated instances of curiosity about just one of the two. The Greek historian, Herodotus, for example, writing in the fifth century B.C., in his second book tells of Psammetichus, an Egyptian king, who wanted to find out which of the peoples of the world was the most ancient. His experimental method for determining this was to discover the oldest language, which, he thought, would be a sure indication of the oldest race. To do this, he placed two newly-born children, of poor parentage, in solitary confinement but for the care of a shepherd, with strict orders that no one should utter a word in their presence. He assumed that, when they were due to speak, having received no external stimulation from contemporary language, they would revert naturally to the world's first. After two years, the children began constantly to repeat an utterance *bekos* in the presence of the shepherd, who immediately reported this to the Pharaoh. Psammetichus, upon making inquiries, discovered that this was the word for "bread" in Phrygian, a neighbouring language. The unavoidable conclusion for him, therefore, was that this language *must* have been the world's original tongue, and that the Phrygian race was more primeval than his own.

Now the reality of language development, as determined by more recent scholarship, will be discussed below in Chapter III.

This experiment, though, even if the conclusions were palpably invalid,[1] does at least testify to the power the problem exercised from the beginning. And information of a similar kind survives in legend, sacred book, folk-tale and ancient document in many other countries. In relatively recent times, James IV of Scotland is reputed to have carried out an identical experiment, and proved that a child "spak very guid Ebrew"! And the post-Renaissance period in Europe is filled with like speculation.[2]

Closely tied to this, of course, was the issue of what exactly the origin of language was. Most primitive cultures (and some of the not so primitive) were quite sure that a divinity had been involved from the very start. It is God, after all, who gave Adam the power of naming as described in Genesis 2. 19–20:

> And the Lord God having formed out of the ground all the beasts of the earth, and all the fowls of the air, brought them to Adam to see what he would call them: for whatsoever Adam called any living creature the same is its name. And Adam called all the beasts by their names, and all the fowls of the air, and all the cattle of the field. . . .

And, two verses later, there is evidence for the first etymology: "And Adam said: This now is bone of my bones, and flesh of my flesh; she shall be called woman, because she was taken out of man."[3]

However, almost every other culture has a similar story; the god, Thoth, was the originator of speech and writing to the Egyptians; the Babylonians attributed it to their god, Nabû; a heaven-sent water turtle with marks on its back brought writing to the Chinese; Odin was the inventor of runic script, according to Icelandic saga; and Brahma is reputed to have given the knowledge of writing to the Hindu race. The stock of legend and sacred tradition about the subject is very great: it testifies

---

[1] The fundamental basis of speech in imitation (cf. below, pp. 69 f.) is not disproved by the experiment, if one considers the close similarity of the approximate representation *bekos* to the only sounds the children would have consistently heard—the sheep.

[2] See below, pp. 26–7. There was also the Holy Roman Emperor, Frederick II (1194–1250) who carried out the same experiment; the child, however, died.

[3] All quotations from the Bible are taken from the Douay-Challoner translation (for the Old Testament), and from the Confraternity text for the New.

to the close attention religion paid to language from earliest times, and will be discussed later in Chapter IX.

It is quite likely that intellectual linguistic research started as a result of natural curiosity coupled with a certain wonderment about one's own language. The Greeks, who first developed the study, certainly concentrated on their own tongue at the expense of others in studying etymology, grammar and the relation between names and things (semantics). Foreigners were barbarians, and barbarians babbled. And was not Greek the language of the Olympian gods, embodying universals of human thought in its forms of expression? The fascination of language study began with symbols, *per se*: as early as the fifth century B.C. the Pythagorean school were teaching that every number had its own soul—from which it was an easy jump, a century later, to Plato's ideal, that every name must have one also.

Plato (427–347) has been called the first to consider the potentialities of grammar (πρῶτος ἐθεώρησε τῆς γραμματικῆς τὴν δύναμιν). His conception of speech (λόγος) as composed basically of the logically determined categories of noun and verb (the thing predicated and its predicator) produced a dichotomous sentence analysis which has fathered most systems of grammatical analysis since, whether the parentage has been overtly stated or not. The Greek propensity for speculation becomes really apparent, however, in his dialogue *Cratylus*, the earliest surviving linguistic discussion. Here, semantic problems are given a good airing, rather than other aspects of language, such as grammar or phonetics. The dialogue is in two parts, the first between Socrates and one Hermogenes, who holds that language originated as a product of convention, the second between Socrates and Cratylus, who hold the opposite position, that language came into being naturally, and that there must therefore be an intrinsic relationship existing between a thing and its name. These are extreme positions, and they are debated throughout. Thus at one point it is said: "there is a correctness of name existing by nature for everything: a name is not simply that which a number of people jointly agree to call a thing"; at another, there is the statement: "for nothing has its name by nature, but only by usage and custom". Impasse! But Plato argues the naturalist position more thoroughly: "names would never become similar to any thing unless the things, from which names are composed, possessed originally at first some similitude to those of which the names are the imitations". Etymology is the proof: for example, "Air ($\dot{\alpha}\dot{\eta}\rho$), Hermogenes, is so called because it raises ($\alpha\dot{\iota}\rho\epsilon\iota$) things from the earth; or because it always flows ($\dot{\alpha}\epsilon\dot{\iota}$ $\dot{\rho}\epsilon\bar{\iota}$); or because, from its flowing, a breathing is produced: for the poets call winds breathings ($\dot{\alpha}\bar{\eta}\tau\alpha\iota$)." Other theories are also proposed: that things were originally somehow "imitated" by letters and syllables; and that there must have been a divine origin for language: "a power greater than that of man assigned the first names to things, so that they must of *necessity* be in a correct state" (My ital.).[4]

Modern research has shown that the phonetic resemblance between such forms as those for "air" is coincidental, and it has been estimated that five-sixths of Plato's etymologies, which range from common nouns to God's names, are false. And even granting that half of these were reasonable deductions (remembering the amount of information then available to Plato), there is enough naïvety in the remainder to lead many scholars to suggest that he was being ironical in his views at the expense of contemporary theories. The semantic theories developed more recently which seem to fit at least the majority of the facts are certainly very different. However, whether serious in intention or not, *Cratylus* is still an important monument to a central linguistic dispute—and this in the fourth century B.C.

Aristotle's position was altogether different. In his essay *On Interpretation* he proposes the view, contradictory to Plato's, that language is a product of convention, that there is *no* necessary link between name and thing. To Aristotle, the reality of the name lay in its own formal properties or shape; its relationship to an aspect of the outside world was quite secondary and indirect; "no name exists by nature, but only by becoming a symbol", and again, "words spoken are symbols or signs of affections or impressions of the soul". Under the stimulus of earlier speculative theories, Aristotle looked more closely than usual at the facts of language and its basic structure, and was able to construct definitions of many of the so-called "categories" of linguistic description: noun, verb and sentence,

---

[4] Quotations from Vol. 3 of Burge's *Plato*, 1871.

number, gender and tense—though these were still on a logico-semantic basis, *contra* most modern theories. Throughout, the emphasis is on the arbitrariness of the phenomena: "a noun signifies this or that by convention."

These first ideas thus produced two schools of linguistic philosophical thought, which have since been labelled *naturalistic* (largely Platonist, maintaining an intrinsic connection between sound and sense: φύσις "nature") and *conventionalist* (Aristotelians, who held that this connection was purely arbitrary: νόμος or θέσις "convention"). Both views were based on a metaphysical doctrine which was primarily concerned with the nature of reality; they hardly dealt at all in detailed description of different languages.[5] In their extreme forms, both are untenable. R. H. Robins criticizes the idea of language as convention or "social contract": "language cannot be treated as a kind of code produced self-consciously by agreement between men at a given time. Such a procedure would presuppose the prior existence of language in terms of which to frame the code."[6] The position ultimately implies a first name-giver, who was usually a god. But it is difficult to find supporting evidence for the naturalist view either. Such a theory would allow us to recognize the meaning of words "on sight", but this is not the case. We have to learn the sense of any new word we wish to use. Onomatopoeic words, which are supposed to derive from an imitation of sounds, are also no support, for the few which exist are also largely a product of convention, differing among languages. The dog may go "bow-wow" in English, but in France it goes "oua-oua". And even within one language, a natural one-to-one connection between word and sense is easily disproved by such factors as synonymity and homonymity, collective nouns,

[5] An important difference from modern linguistic method, as was their view that words were primarily *written* units. It was not until later that speech became a worthy object of study (cf. Diogenes Laertius' distinction of *figura*, the written shape of a word, and *potestas*, its value in pronunciation). The word for grammar, γραμματική, originally meant the "art of writing".

[6] *Ancient and Medieval Grammatical Theory in Europe* (London, 1951), p. 8. Diodorus of Megara nonetheless supported the conventionalist position to the extent of calling his slaves by the names of Greek particles!

semantic change and the (rare) cases of sound-symbolism. It was St Augustine who pointed to the obvious inadequacy of the theory, that there are things which make no sound; and the linguist Max Müller summed up the situation neatly in one of his lectures: "the onomatopoeic theory goes very smoothly as long as it deals with cackling hens and quacking ducks; but round that poultry-yard there is a dead wall, and we soon find that it is behind that wall that language really begins."

Of the two, the conventionalist viewpoint is nearer the truth, though a different type of arbitrariness is involved in the name-thing relationship.[7] Both positions, and a third (that there could be a synthesis, a name being arbitrarily but appropriately imposed by a first name-giver) were later developed by other Greek philosophers. Zeno and the Stoics (third century) were probably the last "school" to deal with grammar as a subsection of philosophy, but they were influential in the formation of a more independent linguistic. They established more formally the basic grammatical notions, which have since become traditional in Western thought via Latin. They devised the names of cases, for example, to account for variant forms in the noun. πτῶσις ("case") literally meant "fall", possibly because the cases were seen as having "fallen away" from the original case of the unmarked name (nominative). The accusative (from αἰτιατική) meant "the case of that which is acted upon or caused by the verb"; and so on.[8] Later, Aristarchus, who became head of the Alexandrian library about 180 B.C., was one of many who carried out analyses of the then very different Homeric language. Dionysius Thrax, in the same century, wrote the first formal grammar of Greek, which proved to be an excellent piece of methodical presentation without the older philosophical bias. And there were many others, largely concentrating on the older, "great" literature, and producing an unrealistic doctrine of correctness—that valid linguistic standards had to conform to the language of the ancients.

[7] Cf. Chapter VIII.

[8] The modern label was due to the Roman scholar Varro's mistranslation of the Greek as if it came from αἰτιάομαι, "I accuse". Cf. Bibliography under Jespersen (1922), p. 19 ff. It is worth adding that any attempt to correlate cases with a literal meaning is uncertain because cases usually have a variety of functions (or meanings) in any one language.

To modern eyes, it is strange that all linguistic work should have been devoted solely to Greek, in view of the expansionist policy of the times. One would have thought that a newly enlarged Empire would have provided more linguistic grist for the speculative mill among the alien languages discovered; this was later to be the case at the Renaissance, when further exploration brought increased contact and interest in the languages of South and East Asia and the New World. But no— even the occasional work on Latin is given a noticeable Greek bias. The typical position of the scholar of the time was a normative one: the Greek language had to be preserved as far as possible from decadence. All change was for the worse—decay and corruption. Such a misunderstanding of the facts of linguistic change and of the importance social context has for all language was bound to produce a distorted attitude, of course; but the approach, once it came, remained, and has affected language studies adversely ever since. The Greeks (especially after the Alexandrian school) concentrated study on the language of the best literature as a guide to the desired standard of speech and writing for all; they did not realize that such language is, in fact, an exceptional form of language used by exceptional people; and that when one studies language, the most realistic place to start is the common speech of the majority, against which one can afterwards compare the careful speech of the few—if such a colloquial norm was realized, the Greeks dismissed it as trivial.

THE ROMANS AND INDIANS

Thus a detailed but comprehensive description of the pronunciation or structure of Greek (or any other contemporary language) was not forthcoming at this stage. Nor is it to be found in the work of the Roman authors, who largely followed Greek precedent in a speculative approach to language. Most, indeed, did no original work on Latin at all, but rather chose to apply Greek descriptive categories and terminology to their own language without change. Naturally there was misrepresentation, though the similarities between Greek and Latin made the marriage easier than was later to be the case when the Latin framework was in its turn applied wholesale to many European languages. The important exception to this tendency produced the most influential work: Varro's *De lingua latina* codified Latin grammar under the headings of etymology, morphology and syntax in twenty-six books (though less than a quarter of these survive). Varro's ideas are remarkably modern: his description is largely independent of Greek preconceptions, and he considers such important formal differences between the two languages as the presence of a sixth case (the ablative) and the absence of a definite article in Latin. He also emphasizes the social basis of language, that language is primarily used for ordinary communication between people; only secondarily is it supposed to be a tool of logical analysis and description—a point of view that had been forgotten by scholars then, and which has continued to be forgotten by many since.

Then there are other famous names which should be mentioned even in such a brief survey as this, largely concerned with the two main fields of discourse, grammar and rhetoric. There is Cicero's stylistic work, Quintilian's influential *Institutio Oratoria* on usage and the rhetoric of public-speaking; Julius Caesar on grammatical regularity; and from the third century onwards there were many grammatical works, largely based on the old traditions with the emphasis on philosophy and literature, and often little more than compendia of older views. There is the occasional piece of original thinking, such as when Remius Palaemon established a new part of speech, the interjection; but the majority of authors were exegetes in grammar, not pioneers, as the Greeks had been. In the fourth century, Aelius Donatus wrote a grammar which was used right into the Middle Ages, and a popular book evidently, in view of the fact that it was the first to be printed using wooden type—it even had a shorter edition for children. Then there was Priscian in the sixth century providing another popular grammar: his *Grammatical Categories* is in twenty books, of which eighteen are devoted to the parts of speech. It is the most complete extant grammar of the age we have.

The Graeco-Roman influence on Western linguistic thought, then, consists of a philosophical awareness of language, a working grammatical terminology, an unscientific etymology, a few relatively untested grammatical procedures, and perhaps

a sense of respect for language. There was little else.[9] In particular, there was none of the minute descriptive analysis done on
either language as had been characteristic of the Indian linguists
of the time. In India, techniques were being developed which
could have been of great influence had they only percolated into
the Western world. When they did, in the early nineteenth century, the reverberations were great. But at this time, the focus of
attention was on specifically Indian matters, and their work
consequently remained unknown outside of India for generations. The stimulus for their study was quite different from their
Classical counterparts. The Hindu priests had begun to realize
that the language of their oldest hymns (the earliest being in a
language since called Vedic Sanskrit) had slowly but surely
begun to diverge from their own usage, in pronunciation and
grammar. Now this is a common enough linguistic fact, that
languages are continually though gradually changing, but it had
particular point for the priests and scholars of old India; for an
important part of their belief was that certain religious ceremonies, to be successful, needed to reproduce accurately the
original pronunciation and text of the hymns used therein.
Change was not corruption, as in Greece, but profanity.[10]
Till then, of course, the state of the older language had been
sufficiently similar to the language of the users for the texts to
be passed verbally from generation to generation without fear
of any spuriousness; but this situation could not continue, when
differences were accumulating and providing a substantial
barrier for the priests and the future learners. The solution was
to write the facts down clearly, that is, describe the grammar
and pronunciation of the old language. In this way there would
be an authoritative text, one not bound down by the vagaries of
an individual's memory. The earliest evidence we have of this
feat is the work carried out by the grammarian Pāṇini in the
fourth century B.C., in the form of a set of about 4,000 aphoristic statements known as *Sutras*. This has since been the basis
for large numbers of commentaries (in particular by Patañjali

[9] For the period as a whole, see Bibliography under Allen. There is
no major addition to classical views from about the fifth century A.D.
onwards.
[10] A similar situation was to arise later in Hebrew, for which see, in
this series, *Sacred Languages*, p. 20. Cf. also early Arabic and the Koran.

in the second century B.C.), the scope of the description has widened, to include the whole of the upper-caste register of language, and most linguistic study ever since has been in the form of an expansion or commentary on these early works—a quite different tradition from the Graeco-Roman ideal.[11] Modern linguistics unites both strands, Classical and Indian, and has a speculative as well as a practical side.

[11] Although this is not to say that the Indians ignored speculative problems completely. Sanskrit has terms correlating with the Greek φύσις and θέσις : *nitya* and *kārya*; and the discussions on *vāk* ("speech") are far-reaching—see P. Chakravarti, *The Linguistic Speculations of the Hindus* (Calcutta, 1933).

CHAPTER II

A MILLENNIUM OF
AMATEUR OBSERVATIONS

BEFORE THE RENAISSANCE

Sometime very early on in the history of man came the event which caused the need for Bible translations, world languages, comparative studies, and all the speculation as to the origins and nature of language: Genesis 11 relates the story: Babel, where "the language of the whole earth was confounded". Christ, who has been called the healer of divisions of all kinds, has been the only one to attack Babel successfully. Before the days when the Church had a language in any way official, he had sent the apostles on their mission with the charism of tongues: "And they were all filled with the Holy Spirit and began to speak in foreign tongues, even as the Holy Spirit prompted them to speak" (Acts 2. 4). While the exact nature and extent of the miracle is unknown, it is sure that only some of the disciples had this special gift. For the most part, a new country meant a painstaking study of the way people spoke, with no book to help. It was usually the case that the missionaries themselves wrote the first grammars and introduced writing. Pius XI, in 1933, when the Third International Congress of Linguists was meeting in Rome, emphasized the importance language study had for the missions, and pointed out the ancient nature of this service.

After the first century, the main missionary linguistic activity was to translate the written scriptures into the local vernacular: for example, there survives Wulfila's Gothic translation dating from the fourth century, the Armenian Bible from the fifth, and parts of both Testaments find their way into Old English, in both verse and prose, from the eighth. But by the end of the first millennium, Latin, largely under the aegis of the Church.[1] had become the medium of educated discourse and communication, particularly at the international level. Correct pronunciation was essential, and a high standard of correctness was maintained. The Benedictine Rule, for example, heavily punished the mistakes of children in Latin classes, and G. G. Coulton tells of the devil Tutivillius, who was "specially deputed to collect the fragments of speech which drop from dangling, leaping, dragging, mumbling, fore-skipping, fore-running, and overleaping monks".[2] The Latin Vulgate vied with the Classical authors as the model of excellence to be followed, which unfortunately led to sincere but irrelevant argument when the fact of language change between Homer and Jerome was noticed—an early instance of an apparent conflict between science and religion.[3]

By the Middle Ages there had been an important change in the grammatical tradition. It was recognized that Latin was no longer a native language for the majority of its prospective users, and accordingly the grammar-books became less sets of facts and more sets of rules (that is, less descriptive and more prescriptive), laid out very carefully and simply in many cases. The standards were still high, of course: one current definition of grammar was *ars bene dicendi et bene scribendi* ("the art of speaking and writing well") and in the age of humanism it was the ideal of many authors to write Latin like Cicero. The important position Latin held could also be seen in the Classical orientation given to grammar and rhetorical studies, which formed two-thirds of the Scholastic *trivium*. Grammar to many was the basis of all arts. But the philosophical bent of the ancients was still present—dialectic was the third part of the trivium. This situation was to develop to extremes with the ideas of the group of scholars known as "Modistae". To them, it was the philosopher who was the only

[1] Cf. below, Chapter XI.
[2] *Five Centuries of Religion* (Cambridge, 1923), II, p. 88.
[3] Cf. Abbot Smaragdus of Saint-Michel in the ninth century: "I disagree with Donatus because I hold the authority of the Scriptures to be the greater" (quoted in Robins, *op. cit.*, p. 71).

one entitled to decide on grammatical judgements (cf. the famous maxim *philosophus grammaticam invenit*) because there was one universal grammar in reality which was based not on language form but on reason's laws. The formal linguistic differences (which are, in modern eyes, the only stuff of grammar) were held, paradoxically, to be only "accidental properties" of grammar. Classical Latin was the only logical kind of human speech, as it embodied such universal laws of thought; grammar, in fact, was *De modis significandi*—that is, a matter of semantics!

This was one linguistically unfortunate side-effect of the quite natural concentration on Latin. There were others. With the notion that Latin was somehow an ideal language to which all other tongues should conform buzzing in scholars' heads, there resulted distorted linguistic descriptions of many of the languages which were being discovered in new worlds throughout the period. With new information to hand, but an old methodology of analysis, the characteristics of each language were forced into a Latin mould. And as not even all Latin was held to be good, small wonder that the venaculars failed to live up to the high aesthetic standards of correctness, which exercised a highly constricting influence on the use of languages. If there was a natural law of correctness, then should not grammars be normative, and tell people how they ought to speak with authority? Such a law was almost self-evident, it was felt. Were not languages corrupted by the commoners and preserved by the educated? And was not the preservation of the Classical tongues, in all their early excellence, the main task of the literate? Thomas Elyot in *The Scholemaster* (1570) has this to say: "the providence of God hath left unto us in no other tongue save only in the Greek and Latin tongue, the true precepts, and perfect examples of eloquence". For a millennium, vernaculars were held to be inferior: the favourite adjectives for English in the sixteenth century, for example, were "barbarous, base, rude, gross, vile and uneloquent". Spanish and French were simply examples of much-decayed Latin; and no one until the nineteenth century paid much attention to similarities existing between languages. Dictionaries were also extremely selective, and did not purport to describe all word-usages (like modern dictionaries do) but only the words used by the "best" authors.

It took time for English to become a language of education. Latin was often concentrated on in the schools to the exclusion of other subjects, and it was the focus on Latin grammar, of course, which produced the name "grammar schools" (cf. Danish *latinskole*).

Finally, Latin continued to be taught almost completely as a *written* language. Now this is a common misconception, which puts the linguistic cart before the horse. Speech and writing are different media of expression, but speech is primary: writing is a reflection of speech, always. We learn to speak before we read, alphabets are based on sounds or sequences of sounds, and there are many living languages in the world which have never been written down yet. Mistaken priorities, then, resulted in an "eye-philology" which produced such situations as in the sixteenth century, when French and English scholars could not understand each other's spoken Latin—a difficulty which has arisen many times since.

AFTER THE RENAISSANCE

The period labelled the Renaissance had a number of linguistic side-effects. Geographical exploration and largely Catholic missionary activity brought more languages to the notice of the world, especially in Africa, China and India, and more international economic and political developments demanded better techniques of communication. New discoveries of foodstuffs and raw materials in other cultures brought large numbers of alien words to Europe at the same time as scientific developments were producing new phenomena to be described, for which Latin and Greek terms proved valuable. Europeans, for the first time, became actively interested in language learning. Printing had matured sufficiently to make word-lists, strange alphabets, dictionaries and early grammars available to the interested scholar. Information about languages began to accumulate; translations multiplied and polyglottism flourished; scholars began to study Coptic and Gothic, and attempts were made to survey all the languages known to exist. In particular, there was a renewed interest in Greek, Hebrew and Arabic, which was a great stimulus to biblical studies. In the Middle Ages, almost all Western textual work had been based on the

Latin Vulgate; but after the fall of Constantinople, older texts and commentaries (and traditions of grammar) became available.

Needless to say, the metaphysical basis of grammar obtained a new lease of intellectual life. Partly as a result of this, and partly because of the biblical tradition and status, the old Classical controversies about the oldest language returned, and the position of Hebrew was maintained by many.[4] The sixteenth century saw many proofs proposed for this. If Hebrew was oldest, then it had to be demonstrated that all living languages were variations upon it—which led to the working-out of many elaborate permutations of letters between words of different languages that showed even a partial similarity in sense, to try and prove this causal relationship. One justification for this letter-juggling was that Hebrew was written from right to left, whereas other languages went from left to right! Later, Voltaire was one who voiced his scepticism of such deductions: he defined etymology as a science in which the vowels count for nothing and the consonants for very little.

But there were others at this time who, more patriotically, proposed their own language as the world's original. The Swede, Andreas Kemke, supported the view that in Paradise Adam spoke Danish, the serpent French, and (of course) God spoke Swedish. J. G. Becanus (1518–72) typified the contemporary Teutonic mania for praising all things German by arguing the position of German as the primeval tongue of mankind. His argument, basically, was that the first language must have been the most perfect, and as German was superior to all other languages, then it must have been the first. Historically, German was the language Adam spoke in Eden. It missed Babel, because the early Germans (or Cimbrians) were not assisting in the construction of the Tower. God later caused the Old Testament to be translated from the original German (unfortunately no longer extant) into Hebrew. Charles Butler was one who opposed this view strongly, and supported Hebrew; and then there was always the antiquarian spirit of post-Restoration days, at which time one John Webb opted for Chinese.

However, despite the mass of new information about

---

[4] Cf. above, p. 13.

languages, and the many discussions about the fact of language itself, there was little methodical classification imposed on the facts. Interest in languages was accidental and haphazard, with no effort being made to systematize observations or work methodically through the recorded material. Thus many strange decisions were made: for years Persian was seen as a Germanic language and Lithuanian as a kind of Latin. In 1599, Scaliger made a fourfold division of European languages, according to their word-types for "God" (*deus, theos, bog and gott*) with no further linguistic support. Terminology and procedures were taken almost completely from Classical sources. Linguistics as a scientific discipline did not begin to be formulated until well into the nineteenth century, although there were individuals (for example, Leibniz) who made influential statements in the meantime.

ON THE ORIGINS OF LANGUAGE

During the eighteenth century, the movement away from Latin towards the vernaculars increased in momentum and importance. It reached its apotheosis as a characteristic of romanticism in Europe, to use "language really used by men".[5] The discoveries of the languages of primitive peoples was another factor in this concern for a natural view of language phenomena. One important result of this new attitude was to reawaken interest in the perennial problem of an original language. The Classical discussion had provided little positive information, and the eighteenth-century theorizing of such men as Rousseau, Condillac and Herder was also very vague and subjective. But this was only to be expected. The modern view is that the whole issue is a "pseudo-problem"; being unverifiable, it is therefore not worth discussing, and should only be brought up in historical surveys of linguistic study. The linguist, W. D. Whitney, once commented that "the greater part of what is said and written upon it is mere wordy talk", and just over fifty years ago, the Linguistic Society of Paris made a standing order barring papers on the origin of language from its meetings. This was partly a sign of the times (coming after a century of vague theorizing), and partly because of the absence of any

[5] Wordsworth, 1800 *Preface*.

evidence that could suggest an answer. New information about languages showed no signs of a primitiveness that could be taken as a hallmark of an early or original tongue; and such scholars as E. Sapir consistently emphasized the view that to call languages "primitive" was a misnomer: "We know of no people that is not possessed of a fully developed language. The lowliest South African bushman speaks in the forms of a rich symbolic system that is in essence perfectly comparable to the speech of the cultivated Frenchman".[6] And the comparative method (see Chapter III) had shown in its earliest reconstructions that the further back one went in time, the more complex language seemed to become (not, as the primitivists claimed, the more simple).

But despite such scepticism, the problem has always exercised (and still does) a fascination on the human intellect to fill this gap in knowledge.[7] There have been four main conceptions of the original nature of language running throughout history under various names: language as the creation of God or a god; language as a naturally determined logical relationship between words and things; the psychological theory that mental processes produced speech forms; and the more recent biological view, that speech resulted from the interplay of bodily and environmental forces. A number of interesting, if abortive theories have been neatly labelled and deserve mention. The echoic (or "ding-dong" theory) was based on the naturalistic imitation conception—the sounds of language originally reflected the objects. Another onomatopoeic theory was nicknamed the "bow-wow" theory, for here speech sounds were said to have developed from man's imitation of animal noises. The "pooh-pooh" theory put the case for the instinctive development of sounds from exclamations and emotional cries; and the "yo-he-ho" theory suggested a correlation of speech with the vocal accompaniment that was supposed to accompany physical effort, especially when of a rhythmical nature. More recently, there has been proposed a "yum-yum" (or "ta-ta") theory, which postulates that sounds were originally a kind of

---

[6] *Language* (New York, 1921), p. 22. Cf. also Quirk, *The Use of English* (London, 1961), pp. 39–42.
[7] See, for example, A. S. Diamond, *The History and Origin of Language* (London, 1959).

gestural response, the combination of mouth gesture and air current producing sounds which were gradually conventionalized.[8] We have what Thorndike has called the "babble-luck" motif, which is in line with one theory of language learning, and implies the habitual recognition of arbitrary symbols to produce similar responses in individuals—a behavioural theory of linguistic reinforcement. And finally, there is Sturtevant's suggestion that the origin of language *must* have been in telling lies! [9]

Such haphazard origins have scholars given to speech. None of the theories accounts for anywhere near the total data of any language, if one measures them by available evidence today; and the impossibility at the moment of ever finding criteria to judge the original position has been a major cause of linguistic scepticism. The implications of the divine theory are interesting, however, despite the fact that it is usually criticized as a more primitive explanation, because its acceptance calls for no reasoning, just faith—the analogy is with the *deux ex machina* of Classical tragedy. The theory has been alive a long time: Plato talks of the power "greater than that of man" who "assigned the first names to things"; and Bishop Wilkins in 1668 said "that the first language was con-created with our first Parents, they immediately understanding the voice of God speaking to them in the garden". The biblical account in Genesis 1 does not provide an answer, though there are some hints. It implies that God had the power of naming from all time: he brought the beasts to Adam "to see what he would call them". Philo Judaeus thought that this must have been some kind of test. And certainly the power of expression is present long before Adam, if one takes the anthropomorphic language of the inspired writer as a guide: "And God said: Be light made". Of course the Hebrew verb of saying was the obvious choice for the idea involved here, and it is distinct from the verb of naming which Adam uses later. It would thus seem that the power of naming was resident in God, and one of Adam's gifts which he utilized when given the opportunity. But whether this

[8] See Sir R. Paget's work; for example, *Babel, or the Past, Present and Future of Human Speech* (1930). Also see Darwin's *The Expression of the Emotions*, and, at the very beginning, *Cratylus*.
[9] Cf. E. H. Sturtevant, *An Introduction to Linguistic Science* (Yale, 1960), pp. 48–9.

gift was a latent ability that developed along the lines of one of the above theories or not, there is no mention—nor is it theologically important. The important point is hardly whether God created human speech directly or allowed human beings to evolve it by any of these hypotheses, but rather that the intellect without which speech cannot exist must itself be of divine creation.

The whole subject has been recently reviewed by a linguist, C. F. Hockett. In an article on "The Origin of Speech"[10] he compares human speech to the communicative systems of other animals, his purpose being to distinguish what characteristics human speech has that other animal "languages" have not, in the hope that this will point to "stages" in the development of the one from the other. Such an evolutionary procedure may not convince, but his technique of differentiation is well worth studying for its own sake, testifying as it does to the uniqueness of the human faculty and hence of the human mind. Hockett is looking for "the basic features of design that can be present or absent in any communicative system, whether it be a communicative system of humans, of animals, or of machines". To this end, he sets up thirteen design-features which are characteristic of *all* human languages, but which are absent in different proportions from animal systems. The relevant animals he chooses to study are those which have had "languages" of sorts attributed to them over the past few years: bee-dancing (showing direction and source of nectar), stickleback behaviour during mating, herring-gull postures which indicate basic biological impulses, call-notes of birds and gibbon calls.

There is a clearly instinctive basis for all these activities: the biologist, Lorenz, talks of "releasers" in this connection, that is, simple patterns in the environment which operate a releasing mechanism innate in the animal's brain; and in so far as communicative behaviour is an act which stimulates a response in another animal, then these are all instances of communication. But all communication is not language (see Chapter IV), and the point here is, How far do these activities differ from human speech? Or, to rephrase the question, What are the characteristics of human speech which make it different from any other

[10] *Scientific American* (September, 1960).

kind of communicative behaviour? It would seem that four design-features are of crucial importance:

(a) "Displacement", which allows man to talk about things removed in space or time. Animals need an immediate stimulus: they cannot "talk" about the past or future; only about what is happening.

(b) "Productivity." Animals have a very finite range of communicable signs which cannot be extended naturally and cannot be used outside of the specific biological situation which gave rise to it. The communicative behaviour of two members of the same species is the same. Humans, however, have a near-infinite source for language forms; there are more sentences in human language than anyone could ever say, and few people know more than one-tenth of the words in the Oxford English Dictionary. But each has the capacity to extend his linguistic knowledge or construct new and recognizable sentences, by utilizing the store of information which is reflected in grammars and dictionaries. We can be consciously creative; animals cannot.

(c) "Traditional transmission." Although the capacity for language acquisition is present in the genetic code of each of us, any language has nonetheless to be learned conventionally. We learn to speak the hard way, after making many mistakes. It is this arbitrariness which allows us to say so much, in fact; if we were tied down to what was given to us via heredity, or to the influence of our immediate environment, there would be little room for language change or creativity. But with the animals mentioned, the instinctive basis of their communicativeness means that it can never develop beyond the few biologically important functions it has always been linked with, and which are passed on from generation to generation. Translation does not exist in the animal world; for them, Babel does not apply.

(d) "Duality of patterning." This simply means that human speech displays a complex structure lacking elsewhere. Items function in our speech at different "levels"; [11] for example, separate sounds on their own are almost always meaningless, but when they are grouped together into words, they become part of a higher unit of structure, the word, which has meaning.

[11] For the concept of level, cf. below, p. 79.

This is important, because without some kind of structuring, we would not have the memory to assimilate and reproduce the thousands of symbols relevant for all our potential messages. Twenty-six letters give us half a million words in English, which we can read fairly easily; but if each word was like a new letter, language learning would be very limited. Animal "language", on the other hand, works without structure; the signs are self-sufficient, instinctively produced and iconically functioning.

Such positive characteristics, then, are the main reason for distinguishing animal from human speech. Any other form of "language" can be shown to be either a metaphorical expression (as in the "language" of music) or an analogous usage (as in the "language" of machines). Human speech is undoubtedly unique, and a suitable attribute for the uniqueness of man. How this developed to its present complexity from the more primitive forms of hominoid apes is likely to remain a vain question. Biological research has shown that there are physiological differences existing between animals and man in the brain which reflect the mental division and cast some light on the naming process. It seems that only in man is there a direct link between the sight area of the brain and the other organs of sense; in animals, the link between sight and sound (or touch) is made via the appetite: which is what Pavlov with his dogs, and other animal behaviourists would lead us to suggest. But, again, there is no explanation deducible as to the origin of this difference. And from the point of view of religion, all one can say is that there is no contradiction between the biological and linguistic facts, on the one hand, in so far as they are known, and the factual or metaphorical account of the linguistic situation as given in the first chapters of the Bible, on the other.

CHAPTER III

THE NINETEENTH-CENTURY PROFESSIONALS

THE DEVELOPMENT OF THE COMPARATIVE METHOD

Scholars and kings have been attracted to studying the curiosities in language for generations, but only recently have the former begun to concentrate on a more systematic survey of the main similarities and differences between language forms and introduced important general principles, such as the concept of language change. Earlier study, as the above chapters have suggested, was largely haphazard and vague: if the differences were noted, it was often to dismiss them as coincidental or of negligible importance, or (as with the original-language hunters) to mould the facts to suit the required theory; if the changing nature of language was considered at all, it was as part of a natural process of corruption, and measured against the changeless status of Latin. Above all, with the possible exception of some early Jewish scholars, no one had noticed anything systematic about either resemblances or differences. The first to point out objectively the fact of a systematic language similarity was a French Jesuit missionary named Coeurdoux, who showed in 1767, with many examples, that Latin and Sanskrit had definite grammatical and lexical correspondences; but his suggestion was unfortunately not published until much later, and by this time, Sir William Jones had said the same thing

more emphatically, and included Greek and Celtic in his observations. He had had an opportunity of studying Sanskrit in
detail while Chief Justice in Bengal, and in a speech to the
Asiatic Society in February 1786, he made a statement which
was to inspire the basic principle of comparative linguistics:

> The Sanskrit language, whatever be its antiquity, is of a won-
> derful structure; more perfect than the Greek, more copious
> than the Latin, and more exquisitely refined than either, yet
> bearing to both of them a stronger affinity, both in the roots of
> verbs and in the forms of grammar, than could possibly have
> been produced by accident; so strong, indeed, that no philologer
> could examine them all three, *without believing them to have
> sprung from some common source, which, perhaps, no longer
> exists.* (My ital.)

Even though this was unsupported in detail, Jones' impressions were in print, and thus circulated widely. Within the following thirty years, the effects of the stimulus became apparent,
and the reverberations of the theory took over a century to
settle.

The first systematic attempt to study the implications of
Jones' statement in detail was made by a Dane, R. K. Rask, in
an essay written in 1814, called "An Investigation into the
Origin of Old Norse or Icelandic Language". It was followed
shortly afterwards by Franz Bopp's first major work, "Concerning the conjugation system of the Sanskrit language in
comparison with those of the Greek, Latin, Persian and
German languages". This was published in 1816, three years
before a third scholar, Jacob Grimm, enlarged and further
systematized Rask's statement in his *German* (i.e. Germanic)
Grammar. By 1833, the techniques and data amassed by these
three, supplemented by much extra information from contemporaries, led to the production of Bopp's comprehensive handbook, which was extremely popular and went through three
editions: the *Comparative Grammar of Sanskrit, Zend, Greek,
Latin, Lithuanian, Gothic and German* took nineteen years to
prepare, and by its third edition incorporated Old Slavic, Celtic
and Albanian.

The study began in an empirical way within its own field.
However, it was not long before these historical linguists or
"comparative philologists" shifted their focus of attention. They

began to deduce, from the comparative data which was being described, the features of a language which they assumed must have been in existence before the earliest records, which would account for the similarities in the forms of, say, Sanskrit, Greek and Latin. The assumption that the languages were related produced the further assumption that they had a common source. At first it was thought that Latin and Greek had descended from Sanskrit (which had always held a patriarchal position in the eyes of European scholars); but further research indicated that all three languages were cognate, that is, had a common ancestor, which had not survived in any recorded form. Work thus began in determining this old language's characteristics.

It was noticed that Modern Romance languages showed a similar pattern. The similarities existing between certain words and forms in Italian, Spanish and French, for example, also suggested that they came from the same parent-language. The fact that the three words for "father" had so much in common (Italian, *padre*, Spanish, *padre*, French, *père*) would be just one case in point among thousands. But one could then go further, and suggest that the word, as it stood in the original parent-tongue, must have had a *p* in it, because this is a common factor in the three modern languages; similarly the presence of an *r* might be deduced; and if sufficient comparative work was done, the reason for the vowel discrepancy might become clear, and the parent-language vowel determined. In such a way, one could arrive at an ancestor form *pater—which in this case exists*, in Latin. By studying a large number of such cases, dealing with more complex grammatical constructions as well as with letters, the totality of Latin could be deduced, as it were, backwards.

This reasoning, then, was applied to Latin, Greek and Sanskrit, which showed a very similar set of correspondences. Here the forms for "father" were: Latin, *pater*, Greek, πατήρ (*patēr*), Sanskrit, *pitar*. The conclusion reached suggested that the parent-language from which the three had derived would have had a word for "father" of the form **patér*. The asterisk in front of this form, or any other in comparative philology, indicates that it is a reconstruction along these lines which is not attested in written records; in other words, it is no more than a hypothesis, though a very plausible one, because a multiplicity of morphologically similar examples has been considered in the process of reconstruction, taken from as many cognate languages as would seem to be relevant. Thus, in deducing the older word for "brother" (a word with a very different history from "father" despite its superficial similarity) one might well wish to consider as part of the evidence Latin, *fräter*, Greek, φράτηρ (*phrätēr*), Sanskrit, *bhrätär*, Old Church Slavonic, *bratrŭ*, Gothic, *broðar*, Old Irish, *bräthir*, Old English, *brōðor*, and so on—from which one could arrive at a form *bhräter*.

The original parent-language, then, was gradually reconstructed, word by word, as far as the evidence of the written remains allowed, and is now called Proto-Indo-European (or PIE for short). It was assumed that it was being spoken before 3000 B.C. The languages which developed from it were thus called the Indo-European family, according to the then popular model of linguistic description, and the relationship of one member language to another was described in kinship terms: Sanskrit, Greek and Latin were "sister-languages". Such a procedure accounted satisfactorily for the interrelationships of most European languages (Basque being the odd exception) by postulating various sub-families or groups of languages within the main family that had some kind of common structural core. From the practical point of view, PIE was given more attention by scholars partly because there was more written material available in the daughter-languages, and partly because the users of the languages within the Indo-European complex were politically and economically more important. This is, of course, by no means to say that a language of Indo-European stock is somehow intrinsically "better" than any other: a culture may be more powerful than another, but this does not affect the status of the languages used which are, linguistically speaking, of equal standing.

Thus the major language "families" of the world were suggested, and those of Europe given more detailed treatment: the Germanic family, the Romance, the Balto-Slavic, the Celtic, the Hellenic, and so on. Figure 1 shows one way, using the family tree model, of relating the languages of the Germanic group, of which English is a member.

This was the genealogical method of classification. At the same time, attempts were being made to produce an alternative

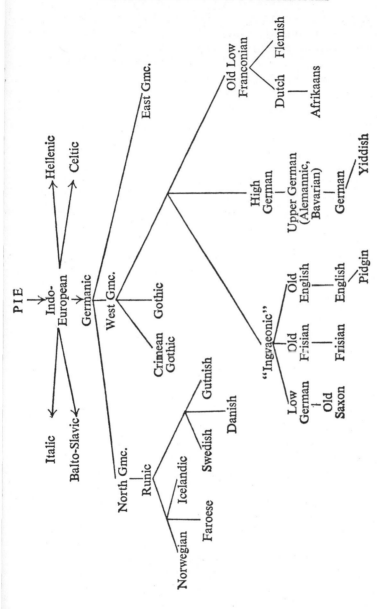

FIGURE 1: THE GERMANIC FAMILY OF LANGUAGES

classification of languages, the typological, wherein each language would be placed according to its major structural characteristics. This procedure (isomorphism) was first proposed in detail by A. von Schlegel in 1818. He suggested that there were three kinds of language that could be determined in this way: at one extreme there were *analytic* (or *isolating*) languages, such as Chinese, which have no inflections; at the other extreme there were *synthetic* (or *inflectional*) languages, such as Greek or Sanskrit; and in between there were *agglutinative* (or *affixing*) languages, such as Turkish or Korean, which strung verbal elements together in long sequences. Despite the fact that most languages fell in between these points, Schlegel's theory had many adherents. It did provide a comprehensive standpoint at least, and showed that there were general structural tendencies in the ways languages indicated relationships. Its main advantage, too, was that it did not require a vast quantity of textual analysis before making its statements, thus being a more useful tool than the genealogical model for classifying languages which had no written records. The two techniques are not incompatible, of course; but for many reasons the genealogical approach remained more popular, and despite support by Sapir and other linguists, no broad classification has yet been produced on typological principles that is satisfactory.

A further eye-catching example of relationship is the present tense indicative conjugation of the verb "to be" in Latin, Sanskrit and Greek: the bracketed forms are transliterations of the Greek for ease of comparison, a procedure which also applies to any Sanskrit examples in this book:

sum	ásmi	εἰμί (eimí)	PIE	*ésmi
es	ási	ἔσσι (éssi)		*ési
est	ásti	ἐστί (estí)		*ésti

The regularity of sets of phonetic correspondences existing in such listings was soon established beyond reasonable doubt, and provided the stimulus that led scholars to suggest lines of phonetic relationship between the languages. Thus, for example, the presence of an *a* vowel in the verb paradigm given above for Sanskrit corresponds systematically with an *e* vowel in the other two. The weight of evidence is therefore for an *e* vowel in the parent-language, the *a* having developed from this *e* by some process of phonetic development. If this was so (and the scholars assumed it was), the process could be described as "Indo-European *e* became Sanskrit *a* and Latin and Greek *e*"; or, in a more simple shorthand: "IE */e/ > Skt /a/, L. Gk. /e/.[1] Such formulas were worked out in great detail and became known as sound "laws". This was originally a metaphorical kind of use of the word "law", because the formulas were only representing what were thought of as very strong tendencies for the sounds to behave in such ways; they were not originally considered as exceptionless laws at all—an attitude to be sharply reversed later by the neo-grammarian school of comparative philologists, discussed below.

It is important to be aware that the comparative method was largely empirical, and (under German stimulation) thorough; it was based on textual evidence, information about speech being deduced from an examination of writing; again, it was primarily concerned with comparison of individual sounds (rather than words, or meanings); and it tried to show the systematicness behind the linguistic variation which it noted—an aim which was not always successful, in view of the fact that insufficient attention was paid to the structural character of the language-states being compared before comparative decisions were made. But such an ordering of priorities (non-historical description preceding historical comparison) was not seen as essential until the next century. Meanwhile, as the century progressed, techniques were clarified, principles were more precisely stated, and a scientific atmosphere became the norm. The historical bias towards linguistic data still remained, of course, and its development is worth studying, albeit briefly, partly because some of the suggestions made were of permanent importance, but also because this background is essential for an understanding of the reaction which produced modern "general" linguistics.

---

[1] The oblique brackets are a linguistic notational convention indicating that the letters enclosed are to be taken as the *phonemes* of a language, that is, as the minimal units of sound which are capable of distinguishing between words in a language that otherwise mean the same. A fuller discussion of this difficult concept is given below, pp. 75 f.

HISTORICAL LINGUISTICS IN A SCIENTIFIC PERSPECTIVE

The remainder of the nineteenth century saw the accumulation of a great deal of information on the history of languages, and, in particular, on the details of Proto-Indo-European. Sanskrit was of the utmost relevance in such work, and was hailed as such by many linguists; Max Müller, for example, in 1868, said "a comparative philologist without a knowledge of Sanskrit is like an astronomer without a knowledge of mathematics". An important reflex of this detailed study, however, was an increasing theoretical linguistic interest which took the newly discovered facts about language into consideration. Scholars began to meditate on the underlying principles which the facts of sound-change and related developments suggested. In particular, there was the growth of an evolutionary attitude to language, stimulated by Darwin's work. If plants and animals have a birth, development and death, then why not language too? Early on, W. von Humboldt had emphasized the fact of linguistic flux, though he was only interested in explaining the phenomenon in terms of the changing mental power of the users of language. It was August Schleicher who first tried to develop such a theory systematically, by synthesizing Hegelian philosophy with the Darwinian theory of natural selection[2]; to him, the typological classification of languages as isolating, agglutinative and inflectional was an example of a Hegelian triad of thesis-antithesis-synthesis. Synthesis being the climax of development, the standard of excellence in language was thus tied to the amount of inflection it possessed: Latin, Greek and Sanskrit were indubitably best on this count, Chinese least of all, and all languages since Proto-Indo-European were in the stages of a slow decay, as the comparative method showed quite clearly that this parent-language (*Ursprache*) was probably more inflected than any of the attested languages.

There is a fundamental objection to this approach. Language has little in common with an organism, such as a plant. It has no separate physical existence; therefore it has no separate life

[2] See, for example, his *Die Darwinsche Theorie und die Sprachwissenschaft* (1863).

or death. Language change resides primarily in the users of the language, and only indirectly, via these speakers, is language seen as an abstracted whole. Language is but one aspect of an organism's behaviour, an activity which is continually changing; it is no more than a set of useful conventions.

There is a further, more specific objection, that if languages like French and English are biologically distinct, on different "branches" of the family-tree, then once they have split up, how could the one influence the other in any direct way? Yet this has often been the case, as is shown by the number of loan-words taken from French in recent centuries by the English. Such theories nonetheless had a great influence on the development of linguistics during this part of the nineteenth century. The emphasis till then had been on philology in its more widely accepted sense, i.e. language study as an end to understanding a nation's culture (in particular, its literature). But with the stimulus of natural science, linguistics came to be studied as a more autonomous discipline, with the suggested status of a physical science. It began to be studied for its own sake. Otto Jespersen calls this the "emancipation" of the subject.[3] It was supported at the linguistic level by further developments among contemporary scholars.

The work of Jacob Grimm and others had already produced a more "mechanical" outlook on linguistic data, with more and more sound "laws" being formulated. But there was still a large amount of material that could not be accounted for, and sound-changes which seemed to be exceptions to the otherwise readily perceivable patterns of development. But when Karl Verner proved in 1875 that one set of unsatisfactorily explained sound-changes could be shown to fit a regular pattern by formulating a new phonetic principle hitherto ignored, a new attitude in linguistic scholarship became apparent; it was supported in other publications appearing at the same time (for example, by De Saussure, Brugmann) that showed the relationship between Sanskrit and Indo-European more clearly. Certain scholars thus began to assume that *all* exceptions were explicable in the same way, that is, that they only remained exceptions because insufficient study had been made of the material to determine the

[3] *Language: Its Nature, Development and Origin*, Chapters I–IV.

underlying principles of development which could be formulated as laws. Sound changes were not haphazard, it seemed: a comprehensive, objective examination of the data, paying careful attention to the mutual influence exerted by sounds, could produce a satisfactory explanation of a regularity behind all sound-changes. "Sound laws have no exceptions" became a canon of the new attitude, held by men who were called by their older contemporaries, a trifle satirically, *neo-grammarians* (Jung-grammatiker). Of major importance in their doctrine was the concept of analogy, as this was the linguistic force which tended to normalize differences in language.

This approach thus focused attention on the physical side of language; but its methodical rigidity naturally evoked some heated criticism. This was too mechanistic an approach, it was said, which left the human being out. Language had two sides, not one: there was form, but there was also function (or usage), and this was the social (or pragmatic) province, which provided the ultimate criterion for language. But this criticism the neo-grammarians ignored.

The criticisms were largely true; the social basis of language had yet to be thoroughly expounded. However, the result of the movement was to inject a greater scientific precision and awareness into linguistics, which supported the tendency to see the subject as a kind of natural science. The perspective was still evolutionary—all explanations continued to be historical in the following years—but there was a more rational, empirical approach to language, especially in its contemporary, living forms, which was first formalized in theoretical detail in the work of De Saussure. The old, fanciful, vague theorizing was gone; reliable major work, synthesizing and codifying the results of widespread scholarship, was becoming available. The comparative method had been proved to be of great use in historical linguistics, and a number of important points had been raised and clarified. This chapter will close with a discussion of some of them.

First, such philological procedures firmly dissolved all the old theories that one of the spoken languages of the world was the oldest.[4] Moreover, it caused further confusion in the anthro-

---

[4] Cf. above, pp. 12, 26.

pological camp among those who maintained that whichever language it was that Adam spoke in Eden, it was sure to have been a simple language; for the comparative method indicated that the further back one went in reconstruction, the more complex the inflections of language appeared to be. Indo-European was much more inflected than either Greek or Sanskrit; and there was no evidence that Indo-European was anywhere near the starting-point of mankind's language. There was a geographic coincidence between the linguistic judgement and the historical, in so far as both sets of evidence pointed to a place of origin for civilization north-west of the Indian sub-continent (which might even fit in with continental drift theories too), but it was all very hypothetical, and how long a variety of Indo-European was being spoken in that place was indeterminable.

Secondly, the method gave further grounds for dispelling the naïve linguistic notion that there were "primitive" languages. The fact that Latin developed into French, this therefore being the "younger" language, is no reason at all for using the adjective "primitive" for the latter, if primitive is to be defined in terms of "lacking in complexity" or "inadequacy". As Sapir pointed out (see page 28 above), *no* language is primitive, because each is equipped, as far as we can tell, to talk about what it needs to. Primitivism is only relevant as a sociological judgement in relation to a preconceived norm, and it is totally irrelevant to linguistics.

Thirdly, one should remember that arbitrarily to date and label language states with different names, as is usual in comparative work, is a distorting process. Language is *continually* in a state of flux; it is always changing. Latin did not suddenly become French overnight, nor Old English Middle English; and it is impossible to pin down the exact moment when any two dialects diverged to the point of unintelligibility, at which point we say they are separate languages.[5] The names given to the various language-states postulated in the comparative method are averages, approximations only, as are the dates. Transitional periods are always present between two arbitrarily determined points.

[5] The information derived from the newly developing field of lexicostatistics may provide greater precision here: cf. Bibliography under Lehmann, Ch. VII.

While one can be optimistic about the gains linguistics has had from comparative philology, it is not to be thought that philology provides all the answers, even within its own field. In the Indo-European family, for example, for a variety of reasons, Basque, Sumerian and Etruscan have no obvious place. And the relationship of Indo-European to any other of the world's great language families (for example, the North American Indian languages, or the Malayo-Polynesian family) is impossible to ascertain in the present stage of study, though attempts, some misguided, have been made. Nor is philology likely to make much progress in this field: with primitive cultures there are rarely any written records and hence no basis for historical reconstruction. It is highly probable that many languages of non-Indo-European families have already disappeared, leaving no trace, and there are many hundreds of tongues that remain unanalysed to date.

There are also some important limitations to the comparative method as such, which makes one wary of relying too uncritically upon it. It concerns itself overmuch with dead languages, and with letters rather than sounds. Secondly, it is preoccupied with the similarities existing between languages, as opposed to the differences, which are probably more important. For example, the method does not allow for independent changes arising within a language once it has left its parent, which might not affect the parent at all; and an attempt to read such new features into the structure of the parent language (as the method is bound to do) can only produce distortion. Thirdly, and more important, there is the charge that the theory embodies a fundamental inconsistency in comparative procedure. The method characterizes a language as, say, Indo-European, by pointing to certain linguistic changes that have occurred in the course of its subsequent history; but in doing this it ignores other changes that have also occurred, which may be equally characteristic. And there is no criterion or principle furnished by which one can explain which type of change is relevant for deducing a parent language, and which is not, and this is dissatisfying. English may be Germanic in one sense, but it is Romance in another, especially when one considers it from the point of view of vocabulary. Fourthly, the method assumes that as soon as two languages split off from a parent, they no longer influence each other formally—which is by no means necessarily true—witness modern Russian's influence on, say, English, or English on a variety of languages. Fifthly, the method fails to consider a variability in the degree of precision attainable at various periods of reconstruction: the further back we go in history, the more time and space we allow in between language states, and thus the more unknown influencing factors. It is not possible to talk of Indo-European with the same degree of certainty as one can Old English, but the sound-laws are poker-faced, and equate all ages in their formulas. And finally, there is the assumption that Proto-Indo-European was a single language which can be deduced from all the forms evidenced in daughter languages. It is rather more likely (in view of certain contradictory pieces of evidence in the reconstructions, and in view of what we know about the nature of language) that the parent-language involved *many* dialects, not just one which has been miraculously preserved in extant languages. But to determine the dialectology of Proto-Indo-European would be a task to wither even the most ardent German philologist's spirit!

The twentieth century brought a reaction to purely historical studies and today the most valuable and alive aspect of comparative linguistics is the subject of *dialectology* (or *dialect geography*), which studies variation in the speech-forms of a language, and thus deals in the state of contemporary languages and emphasizes speech to the almost total exclusion of writing. To understand this unprecedented emphasis on speech and the living language, however, one must now go on to consider the implications of general linguistics, and the more all-embracing science of communication.

CHAPTER IV

THE IMPLICATIONS OF COMMUNICATION

Language is the most flexible and frequently occurring manifestation of human communicative behaviour, which is itself part of the domain of cultural anthropology. It would therefore be a useful perspective to discuss the implications of communication, *per se*, before considering in detail what language is and what linguistics does.

The act of communication involves the transmission of a message from a human transmitter to a receiver by means of a channel. For the purposes of analysis, several stages in this process may be distinguished, which in the actual situation would be gone through automatically and almost instantaneously. In the typical linguistic situation, the transmitter (A) wishes to communicate a message to someone else (B) who is in speaking distance. The concepts that A wants to transmit have therefore "sprung to mind" in A's brain—how this has happened is not relevant to the present purpose. Telepathy aside, direct mind-to-mind communication is not possible; it follows that the mental activity has to be translated into a more readily communicable form, which will be the particular linguistic code that A and B happen to be using. This is done by a mental encoding of the message, utilizing A's knowledge of the language (idiolect) which is stored as linguistic experience in memory: formless concepts are "matched up" with structured linguistic sounds or representations of sounds (letters, in the case of a written, as opposed to a spoken communication). The next

stage is when the message, now discretely structured,[1] is sent
via the nervous system to the part of the anatomy to be acti-
vated by muscular activity—the vocal organs in the case of
speech, the arm and hand in the case of writing. The precise
means of actualizing the mental "figurae" as neurological impulses is not yet understood; there is still a gap between mind
and matter. However, the message still reaches the vocal organs
successfully, and they respond habitually to the segments of the
message (if the transmitter speaks the language fluently) producing sound. The sound activates the air particles around the
mouth, which then set up a wave-like motion in the atmosphere. This continues for a certain distance, depending largely
on the degree of force with which the sounds were uttered. If
one is within this distance (hearing distance), the sound-waves
strike the ear-drum of the receiver (B). The physiological
mechanism then transmits the signal via the nervous system to

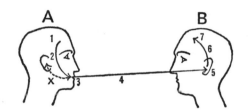

1, Psychological; 2, Neurological; 3, Articulatory; 4, Acoustic;
5, Auditory; 6, Neurological; 7, Psychological.

(X represents "feedback": A can hear his own voice when speaking.)

Figure 2: Stages involved in an Act of Vocal Communication

the brain, where the linguistic message is decoded, the forms
being intuitively measured against B's own store of linguistic
experience (idiolect) and finally interpreted. At this last stage,
certain other non-linguistic factors such as facial expression or
the situation in which the utterance was made might support a
particular interpretation at the expense of some other. The com-

[1] Linguistic discreteness refers to the way sounds and forms of
language are clearly differentiated from each other, and do not overlap
or run into each other in form; they are clear-cut.

munication circuit has then been completed. If communication has been successful, the concepts B has in his brain should be identical to those which A encoded. B has understood.

Such an identity of concepts would be an ideal instance of communication. To be practical, however, certain of the assumptions have to be considered to see just where things could and do start to go wrong. For communication to be successful, first of all, it is necessary that the linguistic code used by A is also that used by B in the same systematic way; if it is not, then unintelligibility will result. This is not simply a question of the two speaking the same language. Even within one language, it is usual to find a mixture of understanding and misunderstanding in any message, for reasons which will be discussed in relation to semantics.[2] The scope of the problem can be briefly indicated by the fact that what a word means to A is not necessarily the same thing that it means to B, although the form of the word does not change. If A is an industrial manager, a message, such as "We are getting automation next month" is liable to mean a favourable situation, because automation, for him, means production efficiency and increased profit. But if B is a factory worker, who is likely to lose his job by this move, the message, as might be expected, signals something very different, and the result could be a breakdown in communication, the cause of most industrial disputes. Similarly, ecumenical dialogue needs to be aware of the ways words are liable to be "loaded", taking on dissimilar meanings in the minds of others for historical and other reasons.

To "speak the same language", then, requires that there be equivalences of many different kinds. On the one hand, the idiom implies that A and B make use of the same stock of sounds, grammatical rules and vocabulary (language inventory); on the other, it means that they do not give widely different interpretations to the same formal message. Successful communication is a more-less probability, that has to take a number of variables into consideration—knowledge of the language by both A and B, the previous experience of the receiver and the general context of situation. Speaking a different language, in both senses, is the most widespread cause of failure of communication; and,

[2] Cf. Chapter VIII.

of course, because no two people's linguistic and personal experience is ever the same, perfect communication is never going to be possible. The criterion of intelligibility rather has to be one of adequacy in normal conversation; one gets the "gist" of the message with more or less precision. Difficulties only really begin to arise when the demand for precision is very strong, as in intellectual discussion of different kinds. Then, recourse is continually had to definition of terms, to iron out the discrepancies in the use of language due solely to the personal background of the users.

Another way in which something could go wrong with communication in the diagram on p. 47 concerns the actual mode of transmission, the more mechanical faults that could occur, causing "noise", a technical term borrowed from communication engineering and used to refer to disturbances which obscure the intelligibility of any message transmitted from a source (sender). Under the heading of "noise" for two people speaking to each other would thus come physiological deformities on the part of A or B (cleft palate, extreme hoarseness, partial deafness, and the like, or deliberate false accents, etc.). At the graphic level, illegible handwriting and bad spelling are also sources of "noise", the result of which is always linguistic confusion to some degree. And, of course, "noise" could come in from outside, as when A and B might be heard shouting above the clamour of a passing train or bus.

All these "environmental uncertainties" accumulate. It is rare that we communicate with no noise around us. Thus, as Cherry says: "It is remarkable that human communication works at all, for so much seems to be against it; yet it does. The fact that it does depends principally upon the vast store of habits which we each one of us possess, the imprints of all our past experiences. With this, we can hear snatches of speech, see vague gestures and grimaces, and from such thin shreds of evidence we are able to make a continual series of inductive guesses, with extraordinary effectiveness."[3] Indeed, it is very difficult *not* to communicate at all, because this store of experience is so very large. A complete breakdown of com-

[3] *On Human Communication* (New York, 1961), p. 12. One of the main reasons for this, *redundancy* in language, will be discussed below. pp. 77–8.

munication would only take place if there was *nothing* in common between A and B in the above situation; then everything one did would be complete nonsense to the other. But such situations are rare, because the very purpose of an act of communication implies a "wanting to say"; to *want* to communicate nonsense is an indication in society's eyes of madness. Difficulty, when it arises, does so despite ourselves, and we then do our best to eradicate it.

The above situation is a minimal communication situation. B is the immediate receiver of A's message, which is sent via a direct transmitting medium, the air. It is of course possible to have an indirect channel, where something or someone comes in between A and B, and this becomes essential when A and B are out of each other's sense range, but still wish to communicate. Such extra stages might involve telephone wires, radio transmitting and receiving devices, the postal service, newspapers, or books. The number of possible places at which a breakdown can occur is thus multiplied. But even if the communicating machinery were perfectly efficient (the aim of the communications engineer), it must always be remembered that built into the communication chain are two weak links: the human beings at either end. *All* communication ultimately begins and ends in human beings, and it is here, as we have seen, that the greatest potentiality for error lies.

This continual return to the human being emphasizes the social basis of communication, that it arises out of human interaction, and is directly conducive to their continued existence. No one can avoid being part of a communication circuit thousands of times a day. There is always something going on in which one is either getting information from someone else or sending information to him. In the words of the linguist, G. L. Trager, "Nothing never happens". Man is a social animal who wants and needs to communicate, and signs "make a powerful social cement" (Cherry). The world is tied together with pieces of telegraph wire: communication has made it ,smaller. A voice can be sent around the globe faster than it takes to reach the other end of a moderately large hall. Communication also inspires reorganization and progress. Government documents and business reports are being re-written to increase intelligibility; teachers are finding that they must improve their methods of presentation rather than their facts; research workers are having to make their highly specialized results intelligible to an interested public; and all social centres and services, from government down, are realizing that they need to become more aware. Above all, church management has discovered the need for communication awareness, and the signs are that it is at last doing something about it; the word has appeared frequently of late connected with such wide-ranging topics as the vernacular liturgy, pastoral care and mass media.[4]

Figure 2 adequately represents the main stages of *any* communication that might take place directly between two persons; intermediary factors can still be allotted their place. Elementary signalling devices, such as flags on a mast, or any remote control system of message sending (for example, traffic lights), also conform to this same pattern. Now meaningful communication is based on a necessary hypothesis, that the item(s) to be communicated has been selected from a set of alternative possibilities, which could be called the *inventory* of possibilities. In the case of language, the possibilities are in the different systems of sound, grammar, vocabulary, and semantics. The point to be made is that unless these different possibilities are present, no information can be communicated at all. Unless there is a system embodying a number of different states, one of which must be chosen to the exclusion of others, I can communicate nothing. There are many simple instances of the way a communication system is built up by bringing in this possibility of extra choices, and hence extra information. If there is a signal standing by a railway track whose arm *never* moves from the horizontal position, the signal can tell us nothing. It will always be in the same state, hence it is totally predictable and does not communicate anything. It communicates (in a weak sense) itself, of course; it informs us that it exists, is or is not beautiful, etc. But the present discussion is using the term "communication" in the sense of providing additional information about something else, and this the railway signal certainly does not do.

By just existing, then, it is not a signal at all, but more like

[4] See Chapters IX–XII below for further references.

the trees or rocks at the side of the track. Only when one introduces the possibility of alternative states does a flow of information become possible. If human beings decide to make a convention, whereby the arm of the signal is raised only when a train is coming, to indicate a free track ahead, then the signal now communicates information, regardless of whether its arm is raised or not. Whichever state it is in, a train either is or is not coming; this it tells us. It is easy to show that the greater the number of alternative states an object can be in, the more information it can communicate. A signal with three possible positions would tell us a corresponding amount more than one with just two; and so on. Thus, the amount of information a sound wave carries when produced by a human being is very great; its potential form allows many alternative states or variables, and hence a large quantity of information.

In practice, communicating systems usually do have many alternative states, but it is only essential that they should have two to begin passing information at all. Primitive societies have long understood that information can be conveyed very satisfactorily using a simple two-state code, for example, drums with two pitches; and more sophisticated beings have worked out a Morse code, and the binary code of the digital computer, with its presence or absence of electrical impulses, along the same lines.

The analogy of the railway signal may also be utilized in other contexts, concerning the way linguistic information is constituted. In the analogy, there were two ways by which one could see "meaning" in the signal—a positive way and a negative. One could say "I see the signal is raised" (positive) or "I see the signal is not lowered" (negative). Both points of view are of value in studying language. Thus, phonemics discusses sounds profitably in two ways. A sequence of sounds, say, *ten*, has an initial consonant *t*. What information does this *t* give? Positive, in that it performs a crucial rôle in the positive act of recognition of the word *ten*—*ten* has a definable meaning; and negative, in that it has a character all its own which satisfactorily distinguishes it from other sounds in the language, and hence other words, e.g. *den, men, fen*, etc. *t* may be described as *not* being *d, m, f*, etc. This latter point of view, strange to the non-communication analyst, may be called the principle of significant oppositions.[5]

The communication chain or circuit is a comprehensive picture of what one assumes takes place. From the point of view of the analyst wishing to describe actual communicative activity, however, this total description is not wholly possible, because in practice one cannot gain any direct access to the stages preceding external physiological movement. In a study of speech, one must start with the vocal organs, as being the first directly observable stage.[6]

It may well be true that the psychologists' viewpoint is valid, and that "the act of communication does not start with the saying but with the wanting to say" (G. Patrick Meredith). But the fact still remains that this is a hypothetical deduction made necessarily *after* reference to the observable speech facts has been made. It is with the observable data that the linguist, or any communication analyst, must begin; the first step is always empirically or operationally determined, by studying the visual movement accompanying the production of language or code, and the form of the language itself. Other observable factors would be the situational stimulus for the message, and the response of the receiver—part of the total context of situation which is essential for the resolution of linguistic or verbal ambiguities.[7]

Finally, what kinds of activity are involved in the analysis of any communication act or message? All activity which can have a communicative value if deliberately utilized as a message can be conveniently broken down into the two categories, linguistic and non-linguistic. The qualifier "deliberately" is im-

[5] Further examples of communication systems, where rules (conventions) are applied to an alphabet of signs, and where positive and negative meanings would both apply, are games with playing cards, traffic signs in the Highway Code, and rank indicators in a hierarchy (e.g. the army).

[6] Electroencephalographic and neurological measuring devices exist, of course, but their information is of a different kind and difficult to correlate with sections of utterance.

[7] This emphasis on observable data is not to make the communication analyst an out-and-out behaviourist: he must start with behaviour, but he may then go on to make other, non-behavioural statements. Cf. Chapter VIII.

portant; it is implied by the term *act* of communication. Unintentional activity is not communication from the transmitter's point of view; it is accidental noise. Unintentional vocal communication would thus involve coughs, sneezes, and so on, and the "voice set" of an individual. Voice set is the permanently present background characteristic in a person's voice, the unique combination of physiological features which produce a recognizable tone of voice. All utterances are necessarily going to have an unconscious element of recognizability. Unintentional visual communication would exclude any twitchings, or other bodily movements of an habitual kind, as also the general physical appearance of the person (the analogue to voice set). All this activity, visual and vocal, might be going on at the same time as a person is communicating, but as far as that person is concerned, such activity is irrelevant.[8] What, then, is the deliberate activity specifically involved in messages? At the vocal level, it is language; at the visual level it is kinesic activity—facial expression and gesture. Of the two, the vocal activity is infinitely more flexible and capable of carrying meaning differences; kinesic activity tends to have a reinforcing rôle, emphasizing certain parts of utterances or resolving the occasional ambiguity. The study of language is the key to the understanding of most communication activity, and it is to this we now proceed.

[8] It is always possible for the receiver to mistake unintentional activity as intentional; but this is just another example of a misinterpretation, cf. above, pp. 48–9.

CHAPTER V

SOME MODERN IDEAS
ABOUT LANGUAGE

The discipline now known as General Linguistics began to take its present form at the beginning of this century. Its stimulus lay in the nineteenth-century approach to language, but its orientation was quite original. While recognizing and maintaining the value of the scientific study of languages, it did not restrict its scope to purely historical matters, but concentrated more on theoretical points of linguistics that had long been neglected. Allied to this was a recognition of the value of studying living languages, as opposed to a preoccupation with their history, and the analysis of empirically-collected data became more important. Also the limited data and limited aims of studying dead languages were of little practical value to modern states of affairs; but there were obviously a number of fields which linguistic research could help. So while recognizing their debt to the nineteenth-century philologists, twentieth-century scholars set a new course.

From the beginning, the new movement in Europe was distinct from its American counterpart. The circumstances of study were quite dissimilar, and each "school" took advantage of the material that lay on its doorstep. The Europeans had a background of comparative historical study, and had amassed data about the development of Classical, Oriental and (to a lesser extent) modern European languages. Based entirely on written records, their deductions were usually made in the light of philology, seen as a procedure for interpreting texts—results were viewed as relevant to, say, biblical studies or literary criticism rather than to linguistic science. Field work in living languages was not contemplated until later in the period, and was limited to the sporadic activity of dialectologists. The only exceptions were the opportunist studies of missionaries and colonial officials around the world, who produced the occasional textbook with various degrees of competence, but often with a Latinate analytical framework.

Such a tradition, then, can be contrasted with that available to American scholars, who had little immediate contact with the Indo-European studies that held the Europeans' attention. Here, linguistic research began by turning to the sources most readily available, the American Indian languages, and the orientation was thus completely different: there were no written records in the case of these languages, and there were no earlier descriptions—hence it was impossible to make historical statements or use writing as the basis for analysis; there was also a distrust of procedures and terminology derived from Classical sources because of early, distorting, Latin-based descriptions. Later, particularly after Bloomfield, there was a rejection of meaning as the basis of analysis and description. This was another reaction from a European tradition that had produced misleading results. The first task of the linguist, it was felt, was to describe all the forms of the language; saying what those forms meant was a logically later activity. The emphasis was therefore on a meticulous description of the individuality of each language's structure, based on the only available source— the living speech activity of the users. The dynamic rôle given to language was largely due to the initiative of the anthropologists, who stimulated the approach from the beginning. Franz Boas, one of the early pioneers, emphasized the need for field work, to get an accurate, detailed description of the human behaviour involved. In 1911, the first volume of his *Handbook of American Indian Languages* was published; ten years later, another anthropologically orientated work appeared, *Language* by Edward Sapir. These two books, and the students of their authors, were the most influential in the development of modern linguistic studies. Their tradition was continued by Leonard Bloomfield, whose book, *Language*, published in 1933, advocated procedures which have been even more widely taken up.

There was thus a simultaneous development in language

studies on both sides of the Atlantic, with neither side knowing very much about what the other was doing. Large amounts of information were gradually collected by the Americans, and principles of study slowly evolved. In particular, scholars were concerned to show how linguistics fitted in with other disciplines, such as anthropology and psychology. In Europe, however, apart from the work of the dialectologists, the approach was based less on speech description and more on theoretical discussion. In 1916, the lectures of the linguist Ferdinand de Saussure were published posthumously by his students as a *Course in General Linguistics*, and the issues raised here have been the centre of linguistic attention ever since; they have been criticized and modified, but their importance to a proper knowledge of language is undiminished. The following is an attempt to indicate briefly what these issues are, while taking subsequent developments in theory into consideration.

SYNCHRONY AND DIACHRONY

In reacting against the totally historical tradition of the nineteenth century (in which he himself had done some important work), De Saussure emphasized the importance of seeing language from two distinct and largely exclusive points of view, which he called *synchronic* and *diachronic*. The distinction is essential. Both study the same facts of language, but in different ways and from different angles. Synchronic linguistics sees language as a living whole, existing as a state (or *état de langue*); this state is the perceivable accumulation of linguistic activities that a speech community makes at any given "moment" or period in time, chosen for examination in its own terms by the linguist—thus he might wish to study the language of Liverpool for May 1964. To do this he will collect samples within that period, describing them regardless of any historical considerations which might have influenced the state of Liverpudlian at that date. Once the linguist has isolated a focus-point for his synchronic description, the time factor becomes irrelevant. To consider historical processes, which is what the comparative philologist would wish to do, is to bring one into the domain of diachronic linguistics. This deals with the evolution of a language through time, as a continually changing medium, *états de langue* following each other in never-ending succession. Saussure drew the inter-relationship of the two viewpoints in this way (p. 79):

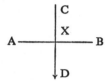

Here AB is the synchronic "axis of simultaneities", CD is the diachronic "axis of successions". AB is the language state at an arbitrarily chosen point in time on the line CD (at X); CD is the historical path the language has travelled, and the route which it is going to continue travelling.

The distinction has been accepted as highly useful by most modern linguists; indeed, it is a necessary distinction, in view of the complexity of language. It would be impossible to study satisfactorily a language system and the history of that system at the same time. Both are subjects in themselves, with different procedures of study and largely different aims. Neither excludes the other completely, of course—there must always be an implied point of intersection—but the linguist can concentrate his study on the dimension in which he is primarily interested. And if he is interested in both, wanting to study some aspect of language from the point of view of its history as well as its exact function in the system of the language, he will still be unable to study both simultaneously, but must choose one dimensions to commence—and this must necessarily be the synchronic. As mentioned above (p. 39), it is impossible to consider the way a language has changed from one state to another without first knowing what the two states to be compared are: a synchronic description is prerequisite for a proper diachronic study. All historical statements imply a valid synchrony. And one of the reasons for the uneven treatment of the facts of many of the older languages by the nineteenth-century philologists is that they did not always appreciate this necessary implication. The corollary, of course, holds: synchronic statements may be the present-day witness of past developments in languages, but such statements to be made do *not* require the consideration of this historical background. It is a point often forgotten by those who teach English in schools, that you do not need a knowledge of Old English or the grammar of the eighteenth century to teach English grammar of 1964.[1]

Originally, then, the aim was to *distinguish* between the two points of view, so that the distinction would be apparent to those who had ignored it hitherto; only later did the focus of attention settle on the point of intersection. The way facts of the one kind can increase our understanding of facts of the other has been a relatively recent discussion point.

LANGAGE, LANGUE, IDIOLECT AND PAROLE

The maintenance of this conceptual distinction resulted in greater attention being paid to the synchronic viewpoint, as the means to the study of language in use. The second major issue, then, was: what is the nature of this behaviour called language? De Saussure had much to say about this too. The confusion about what language is resides largely in the multiplicity of meanings the term has: the Oxford English Dictionary lists ten important but distinct ways the word can be used, and we have already touched upon some metaphorical uses of the word in Chapter II.[2] De Saussure found it necessary to distinguish three useful ways of looking at "language" for clear thinking. Since his time, a fourth has been added.

De Saussure envisaged *langage* (human speech as a whole) to be composed of two aspects, which he called *langue* (the language system) and *parole* (the act of speaking). Briefly, the division is as follows. *Langage* is the faculty of human speech present in all physiologically normal human beings due to heredity, but which requires the correct environmental stimulus for proper development (*contra* Psammetichus, *et al.*). It is our facility to talk to each other. It involves both physiological and psychological factors in the individual, and results in physical, acoustic (or, at a second remove, graphic) activity. It happens to make use of apparatus in the chest and head for the production of sound—apparatus which was not primarily for this purpose. The vocal organs all have other primary functions apart from their incidental value in producing speech (lungs/

[1] Cf. below, p. 82.   [2] See pp. 30–2.

breathing, nose/smelling, teeth/food mastication, etc.). Speech makes conventional use of these organs. *Langage* can never be seen in its entirety, of course; it has no readily perceivable unity of form, being a universal behaviour trait. It is therefore of interest to the anthropologist, but of only secondary relevance to the linguist, who is more interested in *langues* and *paroles*.

Langage is composed of a large number of *langues*, or distinct linguistic systems (perhaps as many as 4,000 mutually unintelligible languages).[3] Now the difficulty of talking about *langue*, as it was conceived by De Saussure and others, is that it was not directly perceivable; it was thus opposed by those linguists of a more mechanistic frame of mind, who refused to tolerate anything which smacked of a belief in a "ghost in the machine". *Langue* was considered by De Saussure to be the totality or collective fact of a language as could be deduced from an examination of the memories of all the language-users; it was a storehouse or "the sum of word-images stored in the minds of individuals".[4] It is now more usefully defined as the complete set of linguistic conventions which work systematically and characterize a given language completely, the static typology of all speakers. As was stated in discussing productivity,[5] none of us knows or needs to know the *langue* of his speech-community in its entirety; this would require the assimilation of all the information in an up-to-date grammar and an up-to-date dictionary. Any particular *langue* is the total social usage of a speech-community which grammar and dictionary attempt to reproduce at the level of greatest generality. As a systemic norm, *langue* has thus two aspects. On the one hand it is based on the actual usage of individuals, and has no reality apart from its validity as a reflector of what is acceptable usage to any given section of society; it has no independent existence, like a Platonic language-soul. On the other hand, it is the hypothetical system on which we base our own usages, and which we teach to others wanting to learn the language. Thus when I say something like "The verb 'to be' has the following forms in English 'I am', 'you are', etc.", I am making a descriptive statement

[3] Cf. below, p. 111.   [4] *Op. cit.*, p. 13.   [5] Cf., above, p. 31.

about the *langue* of English, though the information which was
the basis of this statement could only have been gained from
empirical examination of a large number (as many as possible)
of specific speech acts utilizing such forms. Finally, dead
languages, of course, have *langues*, though how much of the
langue we can reconstruct depends on how much written
material we have available.

This leaves just the actual, concrete act of speaking on the
part of the individual called a *parole*, the deliberate psycho-
physical activity which is what we hear. It is the result of a
personal dynamic social activity which exists in time and in
context, as opposed to *langue*, which exists apart from any particular manifestation in speech. *Parole* is the only object available for direct observation by the linguist; the *langue* of a
community can only be arrived at by consideration of a number
of *paroles*. To study the speech of a single person may tell us
much in cases of psychiatry, aphasia, or speech therapy, but
can tell us nothing for certain about *langue*, which is a systemic
norm based on the usage of a number of people—theoretically
the whole community. The linguist, also, is much more concerned with *langue* than *parole*; but he must necessarily begin
with the latter before he can make reliable judgements about
the former. Diachronic linguistics, then, mainly studies the
history of a *langue* or groups of *langues*. Some behavioural
psychologists have recently tried to study the history of a
parole (linguistic ontogeny), but techniques are very cumber-
some and based necessarily on samples of data only.[6]

Langue and *parole* are useful terms in the linguist's metalanguage, or way of talking about language. The status of the
former, as used by De Saussure, has been justifiably disputed,[7]
but it does not follow that because his conception was unsatisfactory, the term should be dropped altogether. *Parole* on its
own would provide linguistic information of the least important
kind. The linguist wants to make statements which apply, not
just to the speech of individuals, but to the language as a

---

[6] Cf. C. F. Hockett, and others, *The First Five Minutes*, the history of
an interview (Ithaca, 1960), where five minutes of psychiatric conversation takes a large book of reporting—and still omits much of the other
activities essential to communication, e.g. kinesic.

[7] See Bibliography under Ogden and Richards, Ch. I, and Jespersen
(1946), Ch. I.

whole. Such statements are obviously of a different kind from the descriptive statements he might make about separate *paroles*, but they are more important, because it is only against these general statements that recommendations for further usage will be made (as in the language teaching situation). It is plain that the concept of language as a complete system is necessary and accepted in applied linguistics; it would seem that such a concept has some validity in theoretical linguistics also. The linguistic memory-experiences of individuals, and the existence of grammars and dictionaries would provide strong (though not conclusive) support for the notion. On the basis of such evidence, then, it is possible to suggest a use for *langue*, as the highest common factor of all the usages of all individuals in all parts of the speech community. It is the description of a language at greatest generality.

This does not give *langue* any independent existence, because it is at all stages tied to the *paroles* on which its statements are based; the two are not opposed, and there is no dualism. The interdependence is clear when one considers that *langue* can influence and mould *parole*, as when I look up a word in a dictionary and use it; and *parole* can influence *langue*, as when I coin a new word which is accepted by the other members of my speech community. *Parole* is utterance; the totality of utterances makes up usage; and *langue* is based on usage. Correspondingly, all linguistic statements must ultimately be based on usage: *Quem penes arbitrium est et ius et norma loquendi*.

The fourth distinction which has been introduced for un-ambiguous discussion of the subject is *idiolect*. It would seem useful to have a shorthand way of referring to that part of the *langue* of the speech community which exists within one indi-vidual at any given stage of his linguistic development—not his *parole*, because this is the speech act of a moment, but the in-formation (rules, vocabulary) which he personally has learned about the language (*langue*). This is *idiolect*, defined as the totality of speech habits that are theoretically observable in *one* individual. My idiolect is my total command or knowledge of my language. In practice, a thorough study of an idiolect would only be useful in psychiatric or stylistic enquiry, or in distinguishing the speech habits of different people, apart from the evidence of one particular utterance. For example: "Do you know what 'convolution' means?" can be translated "Is the lexical item 'convolution' in your idiolect?" Because no two linguistic experiences have ever been alike, no two people ever have the same idiolect. Idiolect is the result of a long (never-ending) acquisition and assimilation of parts of the *langue* of a speech community.[8] It is therefore implied by speaking, just as *langue* is, and is not amenable to public observation except through specific acts of speech, or some derivative of speech. *Parole* is one manifestation of a part of an idiolect; and idiolect has nothing that is not covered already by *langue*—unless this be personal nonsense, or a secret language which is only intelligible to the writer.[9]

To sum up, then, a linguist can look at the phenomenon of language from a number of different points of view and describe what he sees in his metalanguage. There is *parole*, the speech act of an individual in a specific context, the only observable data the linguist has; there is *idiolect*, which is the habitual patterns utilizable by one individual and derivable from the totality of his speech acts; and there is *langue*, which is the common factor of all mutually intelligible idiolects—the language system. It is the last of these which is the aim of most linguistic descriptions and the basis of most comparative statements. The most utilizable statements a linguist can make are those which have maximum generality of application. *Langage*, the human faculty of speech, is of less interest.[10]

THE DEFINITION OF LANGUAGE AND LINGUISTICS

At this point it is possible to expand and substantiate the generalizations made in the Introduction about what language is, and what, therefore, the primary purpose of linguistics is.[11]

[8] Or, as in the case of bilinguals, of the speech-communities of others. A bilingual is a person who has facility in utilizing two distinct (mutually unintelligible) *langues*; his total idiolect is therefore composed of two mutually exclusive sets of habits.

[9] Cf. the language of certain diarists. To be understood, of course, the code has to be interpreted in terms of *langue*.

[10] Cf. N. C. W. Spence, "A Hardy Perennial: the Problem of *la Langue* and *la Parole*", *Archivum Linguisticum*, ix (1957), pp. 1–27.

[11] It will always be clear, in the following discussion, when the word "language" is being used to refer to "langue" and when to "parole".

It will then be in order to go on to discuss how linguistics carries out its tasks. The primary function of linguistics, it may be said, is to study scientifically all manifestations of human speech in acts of speaking in order to make statements about the language systems (or *langues*) which lie behind such manifestations (or utterances). Secondly, it studies writing, the main derivative of speech. (Other derivatives, such as sign-languages, codes, etc., are studied under the heading of communication, of which linguistics is the major part.)[12] Primarily, also, linguistics studies these matters of language as an end in themselves, to provide extra and much-needed information about what is, after all, a unique phenomenon. It is thus in the first instance a "pure" subject, and its many applications are of secondary importance, though one such set of applications will be the concern of the third part of this book. Linguistics has been traditionally classified as one of the humanities, but this is insufficient for two reasons: it deals with problems that are fundamental to all sciences (problems of expression and terminology, for example), and its techniques and principles have themselves largely derived from the physical and natural sciences—the phonetics laboratory being the best example.[13] Although the subject developed with an auxiliary function, as the handmaid of logic or rhetoric, for instance (see Chapters I and II), it became autonomous during the nineteenth century (see Chapter III) and should no longer be confused with philology, on the one hand, or philosophy on the other. Philology, it should be remembered, does not study language for its own sake; it compares and studies texts of different periods as a means to throwing light on some other, usually non-linguistic aspect of an old society—a kind of literary or historical documentation, and thus one of the potential applications of linguistics. There is an important distinction to be made these days between the work of the comparative linguist and the philologist; the nineteenth-century term "comparative philologist" was a catch-all term that did not separate the two functions. Finally, linguistics is not literature or literary criticism: once again, linguistics may

[12] These aims are based on the way linguistics has been developing over the last fifty years. A more recent theoretical approach is introduced below, pp. 79–80.
[13] See below, p. 74.

study literature as one particular kind (or "register") of language. It is not the linguist's job to say whether a particular style is "good" or "bad", but he can and should be the one to describe it, using the techniques of stylistics.

With the ground cleared, it is now possible to give a definition of language. As is normal, there will be two sides to such a definition, a formal aspect and a functional one. This is not to be rigidly dualistic, because the interdependency of the two in a final synthesis is always an important linguistic consideration. Logically, of course, the formal aspect must be considered before the functional: one needs to know what language is before one can go on to say how it is used. Following M. A. K. Halliday, a working definition is as follows: language is conventionally patterned noise, contextualized. Formal considerations are dealt with under the heading "conventionally patterned noise"; functional definition enters with the word "contextualized", which deals with the way language gets its meaning. These are the main features of language.

Let us take the terms in the formal definition one at a time, therefore. Language is basically noise. Linguistics studies writing also, and even, at times, other derivatives, such as language-based codes, but it is important to appreciate that writing is logically a later and more sophisticated process than speaking. We speak relatively quickly and easily in life; writing comes later and takes longer to learn. Language in the abstract, it has been said,[14] is our facility to *talk* to each other. This emphasis on talking is useful for two reasons: on the one hand it helps to draw the distinction between speech and communication (as in animals or non-linguistic signals); on the other hand it underlines the difference between speech and writing. As Professor Quirk says:[15]

> The use of language primarily and predominantly involves making noises with our speech organs and interpreting other people's speech noises through our ears. It is not a necessary condition of a language's existence that it should have a written form or indeed any form other than talk. All natural languages had a very long history as solely speech before they were ever

14 Quirk, *op. cit.*, p. 37.
15 *Op. cit.*, p. 38.

written down or became associated with rules of spelling and punctuation. Many hundreds of languages exist in the world today which have never been written down yet.

To forget that speech is primary and writing secondary, of course, accounts for much of the misorientated language teaching in English schools, where children find very quickly that the grammatical rules they are taught often differ considerably from the way they speak.

However, language is not merely noise—on a par with train whistles, thunder and the rustling of leaves. It is patterned noise; sound with organization. It will be the business of the following chapters to examine the different kinds of organization involved in language, the different systems that function simultaneously in speech: patterns of phonology, grammar and lexis. The systematic basis of language was also emphasized by De Saussure, who saw the organized totality (or *gestalt*) of language composed of a number of interdependent elements, each of which took its significance from its function in the system as a whole. Without this systematic basis, language could not function; it is evidenced at all levels of language in the rules of spelling, pronunciation, grammar, etc., which we construct out of the language in order to teach it.[16] A rule implies and requires stability and systematicity. Language is not just a carelessly thrown together group of facts; it has structure, items which function regularly in a certain way and maintain definable interrelationships with each other. For example, the pronominal terms in a language function systematically. What does this mean? It means that the oppositions existing between the different terms of the system are consistently recognized and maintained by the users of the system. When I say "he", I do not mean "she, it, I, you, we, they". Part of the meaning of "he" lies in this very fact, that it is not anything else.[17] In a language where the word for "it" does not exist, the meaning of "he" would be different, because there would be one item less to be

---

[16] This systematic approach to language form came to be called "structural linguistics", though this label these days could refer to any one of a number of markedly different "schools".

[17] Cf. the signal analogy above, p. 52.

opposed to. Again, taking an example from the sound-system of English, any phoneme has both a positive value and a negative one: the "p" in "pit" contributes something to the positive recognition of the word, but it also satisfactorily differentiates it from, say, "bit". Yet such recognition and differentiation could not take place unless one was sure of the stable status of the sounds concerned, that they have a regular and definable distribution and character in English from which they cannot depart if intelligibility is to be maintained.

This linguistic equilibrium or homeostasis means that language is predictable in its use. We use language in a largely predetermined way. People do not depart from the norms of usage without exceptional reasons, as would a poet striving to make a new effect, or an Einstein trying to fashion new language to frame new concepts. Normally, imitation is the rule; and though I can break the conventions to a certain extent in the cause for originality in language, I cannot use language regardless of *all* its expected conventions, because then I would be completely misunderstood. The man who talks utter nonsense is classed as a lunatic.

Most of us live by following the conventions of our language. How far these govern and structure our thought will be discussed below (p. 107). The systematicity discussed above is largely due to this conventionality. It would not be acceptable to suddenly twist the expected sound and sentence patterns of English; the conventions of word-order and pronunciation (and spelling), usually called rules, must be kept if intelligible English is to result. But there is another, more important sense of the term "conventional" which was discussed in relation to names and things in Chapters One and Two. There it was suggested that the relationship between words and the objects or situations they refer to is quite arbitrary and conventional. Such a statement could easily be proved by random manipulation of a wireless dial: a sequence of sounds in a foreign (that is, unintelligible) tongue would give you no idea of its meaning. This is not to deny the existence of a few words in every language which have some degree of sound symbolism (for example, onomatopoeia) or which are partly instinctive (for example, some interjections), but the paucity of such words is not a factor in their favour, and even they conform to a large extent to the expected patterns of the speech community. They have to be learned, conventionally, like the rest of language.

Language, then, is systematic patterns of noise used conventionally, in accordance with learned rules; but without a theory of meaning, which indicates how language links up with real events and objects, this noise, despite its pattern, remains nonsense—sound waves without content. Language, to be any use at all, must be meaningful; and it derives this meaning largely from its use in situations. Language cannot exist in a vacuum; it has no independent existence apart from its users. We would never know the inhabitants of a foreign planet had language, unless we saw or heard it in use. Language, as communication, is a social fact; it exists only because groups of human beings use it and reaffirm its meaningfulness by continued use. Semantics studies the relationship which sounds have to context, and forms the introduction to a study of the functional definition of language. These two aspects, what one means by meaning, and what are the main uses language has, will be given separate treatment below.[18]

Before this, however, the logic of the definition requires that we examine more fully the implications of "patterned noise"; the different kinds of function this noise has will then be more readily apparent. Linguistics is one discipline; but it has developed a number of branches which take particular aspects of the patterned noise as their speciality.

[18] See below, Chapters VI and VII.

CHAPTER VI

SOUNDS, WORDS AND SEQUENCES OF WORDS

PHONETICS

All language study begins with single, simple concrete acts of speaking (*parole*). The earliest sounds babies make are monosyllabic cries, the length of one breath or less; then there is a long period of infantile babbling, in which the child gets used to the different ranges and intensities of sounds, and the ways of producing them, via the kinaesthetic feel of lips, tongue and cheeks. But crying and babbling are only a practice period for the production of basic sound patterns modelled on the conventions the parents have been using. Simple intonation tunes come first; then by dint of much repetition, imitation and correction, the child begins to appreciate the communicative potential of noise. The sound-system of the parents is reproduced with extraordinary rapidity; very few adults could master a foreign sound system to the same degree of perfection within the same period. However, until some conscious deliberate use of the sounds is made; until, that is, the baby has learned to associate a sequence of sounds (say *dada*) with the person it refers to, and continually makes use of the sound in this way (that is, names an object), then the sound remains patterned noise only—it has not been contextualized, or given meaning, which is the third essential feature before noise can be called language. The baby "begins to speak" only when he starts using recognizable words in a recognizable (conventional) situation, usually at the end of a year; until then, he is only "trying" to speak.

There are no important cultural or genetic differences in the inherent phonetic equipment of humanity. In the first few weeks of life, children of all races yell in much the same way.[1] But by the time the child has developed an ability to name, he has also become a part of the conventions of his own environment's sound-system, and it becomes increasingly difficult to alter one's speech habits the older one gets. Hence the difficulty for adults to acquire new tongues, and the argument in favour of starting children off on language learning at early ages. The longer we leave ourselves with only one language (our native language), the more difficult it becomes to shake off its influence, at both formal and conceptual levels. There are too many external pressures to bear on the adult, some of them social, some academic; he finds himself analysing rather than imitating. But, of course, imitation is the primary norm for language learning, not the artificial techniques of grammar-translation methods which are still used in most schools. The natural basis of imitation is quite clearly visible in children: the words most repeated are first used, and the child normally has little difficulty amassing a large vocabulary quite naturally and unobtrusively. Putting words together into sentences (grammar) is usually a little more difficult: but there is none of the embarrassment or confusion that normally accompanies adult language learning.

Speech, then, starts with the sound systems of the parents, or (in the case of non-normal conditions) with the sound-systems of those in the immediate environment, nurses in children's hospitals being a case in point. This underlies again the arbitrary nature of language, how it is forced on the individual by circumstances beyond his control; a person's speech habits, as well as his conceptual framework, are both largely imposed; it is only later that we become language-conscious and try to change the *status quo*. Consequently, of course, if there is no stimulus to imitate, there will be no language.[2] The phonetician studies the sounds of speech from a number of different points of view. What he does *not* do is study writing, or letters. Writing

---

[1] For the view that there are genetic factors that differentiate speech groups, see F. Brosnahan, *The Sounds of Language* (Cambridge, 1961).

[2] Cf. R. Brown's discussion in *Words and Things* (New York, 1963), pp. 3–7, of the wild boy of Aveyron, who had had no experience of civilization and hence of language.

is a conventional, visual representation of speech; it is of secondary importance because it is always an attempt to reflect the spoken language for purposes of record or long-distance communication.[3] Phonetics is the study of the sounds of speech as an end in themselves. The only kinds of human noise which are excluded are those which do not function as part of a linguistic system, for example, sneezes, snoring, breathing, mastication, and other "biological" noises. The term phonetics itself has been used in relation to a number of applied fields, such as pronunciation teaching and speech training; but its primary use should be reserved for its function as an academic and scientific study of one aspect of language.[4] In this respect, the following headings are used: *general phonetics*, the study of the physiological equipment available for the production of sounds and the sounds themselves (including *acoustic* and *auditory* phonetics); *descriptive phonetics*, the study of the phonetic constitution of a particular language or language group; and *historical phonetics*, the study of phonetic change, along the lines of sound-laws, etc. The synchronic viewpoint, however, necessarily precedes the diachronic, and is more important in terms of scope and potential application; the following, then, is a brief outline of what is involved in the study of general phonetics.

The act of speech, being one instance of an act of communication, naturally follows the pattern outlined in Chapter IV: a speaker requires a listener, which may be himself, but which more usually is some other person. The communication circuit that is based on acts of speech has been called the "speech chain". Although this covers the same number of stages, phonetics, being an empirical study, in the first analysis, can only deal with the section that is observable—articulatory movement and sound wave. It is impossible in practice, however, to exclude psychological considerations involving the ear of the speaker or receiver from analysis, as will be evident below. Occasionally, it is even necessary to invoke the speaker's opinion on what it was he thought he said, as in deciding

---

[3] Cf. above, pp. 65–6.
[4] Cf. P. Strevens, "Phonetics, Applied Linguistics, and other Components of Language-Teaching", *Volume in Honour of Daniel Jones* (London, 1964), pp. 120–8.

problems of stress, for example; but such are relatively infrequent. The main emphasis of the study is in the mouth and air, studied by articulatory and acoustic phonetics respectively; the reception and interpretation of sounds is the ground of auditory phonetics. Each isolates a different aspect of speech for special consideration; but there is no rigid exclusiveness, and a final synthesis should always be borne in mind.

In practice, the first observable activity in the speech chain is the movement of the vocal organs which accompanies the production of an audible sound. Articulatory phonetics studies the physiological speech mechanism, what it is composed of, how it functions, and provides an articulatory basis for the classification of sound which is more readily determinable than other classificatory techniques. The total range of sounds producible is very large, especially when one considers that the slightest movement in tongue position, for example, is sufficient to cause a difference in the quality of a sound; but relatively precise data can be obtained using X-ray and other techniques: artificial palates, photographs of the inside of the mouth, laryngoscopy, high-speed film and kymography (an older machine which traces a number of simultaneously occurring movements on paper). Careful distinctions need to be drawn between nasal and oral sounds, between vowels and consonants, the different kinds of vowel and consonant, and so on. A full technical description of a sound can be quite lengthy, and each sound which can be given a different description is given an identifying symbol. Thus one arrives at a phonetic alphabet, a system devised for the notation of the sounds of any language in as economical and unambiguous a way as possible. The symbols are enclosed in square brackets, so that they can be easily distinguished from ordinary writings.[5] An important part of a phonetics course is taken up with learning to recognize the whole range of sounds (ear-training) and to produce them

[5] For one basic list of symbols and definitions, along with examples of their use in 51 languages, see: *The Principles of the International Phonetic Association* (London, 1949). A "phonetic language", it should be noted, makes a different use of the term "phonetic": this refers to the way a language's spelling reflects its pronunciation in a one-to-one way; something which does not hold for English, but which is approximated to in Welsh, for example.

accurately, using both imitation and description. The potential subtlety of the differences will perhaps be clearer when one realizes that the two [k] sounds in *keep* and *cool* are quite different, though classified as one sound from the functional point of view, as are the two [p] sounds in *pit* and *spin*.[6]

The reason why so much attention has been paid to techniques of phonetic classification using articulatory methods is that it provides a referential framework which is easy to apply in the pedagogical and corrective fields (including speech therapy). The clearly-defined and clear-cut descriptions are of great assistance whether one is simply talking about sounds or teaching them. But simplification of such a complex phenomenon as speech brings with it a distortion. Speech is a continuum of sound. X-ray photographs and kinaesthetic feel underline the fact that in an act of speech the vocal organs are continually moving from one position to another. They do not jump from one articulation to another as a phonetic transcription suggests; there are glides between sounds, and a number of other alterations which are studied by "combinatory phonetics", when one sound influences another in its immediate environment: assimilation, elision, and so on. Sounds are not naturally discrete; the fact that one hears them so is a function of one's knowledge of which sounds are important in a language and which are not. Most articulatory classification, in fact, supports a preconceived auditory framework. The only way one can really avoid the psychological considerations that enter into phonetic judgements and obtain an accurate and detailed account of what exactly constitutes any given act of speech is to study the sounds using the techniques of acoustic phonetics. It might then prove possible to set up a more objective classification of sounds solely on the basis of acoustic criteria. Since the invention of certain important machines, such a tendency has been gradually evolving. Acoustics is a relatively recent subject, for this reason; the tape recorder was only invented in the 'forties, and most analytic devices have emerged in the last ten to fifteen years.

Sound consists of waves, which are the product of vibration. In the case of speech, this vibration stems from the air stream,

---

[6] The first [k] is articulated further forward in the mouth than the second; the first [p] is aspirated, the second not.

as modified by the upper resonators in the vocal tract. Acoustic phonetics begins by studying what sound consists of, and then what speech sounds consist of: the difference is one of degree only—the latter usually being much more complex than such non-speech sounds as are produced by musical instruments or tuning forks. Sound waves have certain physical characteristics of frequency, amplitude and duration, which can be carefully measured, and which roughly correlate with our perception of pitch, loudness and length of sound respectively. The techniques which have been developed, using machines like the cathode ray oscilloscope, speech stretchers, the sound spectrograph and speech synthesiser—not forgetting the all-important microphone and tape recorder—have resulted in phoneticians finding out a great deal of information about different types of sound and the physical basis for speech. Results are usually presented as visual displays. In the case of the spectrograph, for example, a direct reproduction of the characteristics of sounds on paper is provided, thus making permanent the transience of the spoken sound. These characteristics can then be analysed and measured, and a basis for classification deduced.

The phonetics laboratory is the most obviously scientific part of general linguistics. Its potential use in applied fields has materialized in a number of ways since Bell's "Visible Speech" in 1867; a visible sound shorthand for deaf-mutes is perhaps the most ambitious of schemes aimed at combating the immobilizing effect of deafness. Isolating the exact extent of partial deafness, for example, by audiometric testing, is an essential first step in providing a useful hearing aid. More pervasively, telephone companies have supported much of the research, and utilized the results. Firms which deal in any kind of sound transmission are naturally going to be concerned with such problems as, How much of the sound waves constituting speech does one need to communicate if speech is to remain intelligible? Which parts of a signal characterize a sound adequately? Not everything we say is equally essential for intelligibility.[7]

While recognizing the utility of acoustic research, two qualifications should be mentioned. The acoustic facts obtained may be accurate, but they are not therefore immune to misinterpre-

[7] Cf. below, p. 78.

tation. The objectivity that is given to the findings of acoustics is, in fact, an apparent objectivity only: the facts are only as significant as the observer makes them so, as in statistical decisions. Two analysts can easily disagree about what they see.[8] The acoustic procedure thus brings its own difficulties: there is too much data available for analysis; not all of it is relevant for speech and hence problems of selection and evaluation are imposed on the analyst from the beginning, which means having recourse to context. Language cannot be studied in a vacuum, solely as patterned noise. The second rider is that research is slow and results less widely known than they ought to be because of the high cost of equipment and the lengthy, non-linguistic training which is required before a linguist can utilize such techniques. It is significant that a recent advertisement for an acoustician placed a qualification in physics above one in linguistics.

No matter how clearly I can obtain details of the speech process from articulatory or acoustic research, all results must be subjected to auditory judgements before a sound feature can be allowed a significant rôle in a language. The reason for this is that the *paroles* of individuals utilize so many variables—of pitch, intensity, duration, voice quality, and so on—that it would be surprising to find an exact correspondence between any two articulations of a single sound in any length of utterance. It is almost impossible for one person to articulate any sound identically twice in succession, and different people are likewise distinguishable in minute details, there being a physical basis for voice recognition. But the surprising thing is that despite these differentiating factors, people ignore the sometimes great differences between manifestations of the same sound. Somehow, a *p* sound remains a *p* sound, no matter who pronounces it or where. In trying to explain this discrepancy between a multitude of physical facts and the way people recognize only a limited number of significant units of sound in language, linguists have produced the theory of the phoneme.

Historically, the concept of the phoneme was a product of European thinking, language being seen as a system rather than a group of isolates, but it was eagerly taken over by American

[8] Cf. above, p. 48, and below, p. 178.

scholars, who had long been wondering how to reduce the mass of speech data they had collected from American Indian sources. The early anthropological linguists had made minute surveys of the languages in which they were interested, and had consequently collected data of various degrees of significance without distinguishing between them. The phoneme theory reduced the mass of data by collecting together sounds which were physically distinct, but shared some distinctive acoustic features and functioned similarly in the language: such sound-groups were called *phonemes* of the language. Thus, *p* and *b* are distinct phonemes in English, because they have certain important differentiating physical characteristics, and because in substituting *p* for *b* in the environment—*it* or *cu*—one ends up with words quite different in meaning. This is called the criterion of minimal pairs. On the other hand, the two *l* sounds in *leap* and *pull*, though differently articulated, are not separate phonemes because if one is substituted for the other, there would be no new meaning, just a slight strange accent. The two English sounds are therefore *allophones* or different realizations of the same phoneme, different because the different contexts in which they occur have influenced their articulation. The procedures for classifying sounds (or *phones*) into phonemes are also considered by phonetics, though too detailed to discuss in detail here.[9] An important point is that the phoneme-stock or inventory of every language is different: no two sound-systems are the same. In Russian, for example, the two types of [l] sound are of phonemic importance.

Phonemes, then, are what people think they hear, and their psychological status has naturally caused some controversy. Only recently has experimental evidence for their existence begun to be drawn up. The realistic basis of phonemics has been maintained, however, from another point of view: the subject being called (by Pike), "a technique for reducing languages to writing". But it is not a completely independent branch of phonetics, as it derives its data from acoustic and physiological analysis, and largely governs the focus-points of attention there. Thus, one's views about which sounds are the

[9] For which see Bibliography under Malmberg and Robins. The study is usually called "phonemics", in preference to "phonology", which has a more general range of application, including phonemics.

significant sounds in a language will suggest where to begin an analysis. It is not too much of a simplification to say that phonetics studies the physical nature of sounds, phonemics studies their function. The latter is therefore an indispensable bridge between the "noise" part of our definition of language, and the "organization" part which follows. Phonemics studies the way sounds are organized into units of linguistic form: it looks at problems of defining syllables, the ways phonemes influence each other in connected speech, the functional differences existing between vowels and consonants, and so on. Ultimately it over-laps with any discussion of morphology.[10]

So far, phonetics has been discussed as segmental in character, as studying minimal units of sound; but it is also part of phonetics to consider "supra-segmental" kinds of sound which affect the form and meaning of utterances—formal features greater than single sounds. The main suprasegmental features are pitch, loudness and tempo, covering intonation, stress, and speed of utterance respectively. Silence or pause would also be relevant here. Secondary suprasegmental features could roughly be called marked tones of voice (more precisely, paralinguistic features) which utilize other sounds to make a special effect—as when one deliberately feigns a husky voice over a stretch of utterance, for example. Suprasegmental features are not as rigidly phonemic as the segmental types, though they do have a contrastive rôle, and their forms may be determined with some degree of accuracy. But there is more variation in their use, and there is no rigid one-to-one correspondence between form and meaning, as one has in segmental phonemics. The complexity of their form has unfortunately led to their comparative neglect in linguistic description, but in view of their importance in communication, this situation is improving. Intonation, for instance, apart from being one of the earliest learned features of language, has an important grammatical rôle as well as an emotional one. It can indicate the difference between a statement and a question, for example, as well as communicate whether one is surprised or bored.

The fact of redundancy must also be introduced in a section on phonetics, though it has more noticeable effects on the gram-

[10] See below, p. 85.

matical and lexical aspects of language. One can recognize sounds even after a proportion of their physical form has been removed (e.g. by some filtering technique); not all acoustic information in a sound is essential for correct perception, and some components therefore have more characterizing significance than others. The information one can leave out of a phonetic message while still leaving it comprehensible is unnecessary, or *redundant* information. Communication can take place without it: only the essential sound-features are allowed to pass along telephone-wires, but conversation is still intelligible. Linguistic efficiency as communication does not depend on the perfect reproduction and reception of every segmental phoneme, because of this superfluity of phonetic clues. Again, the linguistic part of an act of communication is normally accompanied by a number of other "cues", residing in the context of situation or the verbal context, which makes even very faulty phonetic articulation understandable. Thus, an example of redundancy due to situation would be if one were to say, pointing at an animal on the carpet, "There's a cap on the mat"; here the utterance would be understood as "cat" because the contextual clues would overwhelmingly indicate that this was "what you meant", despite the fact that the normally phonemic distinction between /p/ and /t/ has been neutralized. Redundancy is therefore due to a superfluity of rules in language, which often duplicate or overlap with one another, and we may therefore omit to follow certain of them from time to time. One cannot break *all* the rules, of course, and hope to speak the same language, but there is a great deal of tolerance, which allows a degree of noise to exist alongside speech without unintelligibility. English, it has been estimated, can be up to 50 per cent redundant—a high proportion indeed.

GRAMMAR

The study of language takes place by splitting the object of study up into several interrelated but formally independent branches, each dealing with a particular kind of language patterning: phonetics considers the way units of sound are produced; phonology studies their organization; and semantics studies the relationship between language and experienced reality. In between, there is the kernel of linguistic study—the different kinds of formal organization that are the subject-matter of grammar and lexis. The term "level" is often applied to the separate branches, emphasizing their separateness, but not implying any one particular procedural approach—one may begin to study a language with the phonetic information, or the semantic, or any other. For a complete description, however, it is usually simpler and more practical to begin with the sound before proceeding to study the sense: having completed the phonetics, one then describes the formal level of grammar and lexis, and concludes with a semantic analysis. This is not the only way of doing things; simply the method which seems most useful in the present exposition. Thus the linguistic field can be summarized as follows:[11]

Object of Study	NOISE is organized into units of FORM which is CONTEXTUALIZED			
	↓	↓	↓	↓
Studied by	PHONETICS	PHONOLOGY	GRAMMAR LEXIS	SEMANTICS

in experience → PHILOSOPHY, SCIENCE, etc.

We now go on to study the implications of linguistic analysis at the formal level.

Firstly, what is grammar, and what is its purpose? It is receiving a great deal of attention from linguists at the present time, as the result of new attitudes to linguistic theory. The reaction is basically against the traditional linguistic approach to language analysis, which derived from the early anthropological linguists and reached an influential synthesis in Bloomfield's *Language*. This older view of grammar was to see it as one kind of speech behaviour, which was to be described as methodically as possible, using speech data derived from selected language users (a corpus), and supplemented by additional information until it seemed there were no further patterns to be accounted for. The description would then characterize

[11] Cf. M. A. K. Halliday, "Categories of the Theory of Grammar", *Word*, 17 (1961).

the language adequately, that is, all possible sentences and their structures acceptable to the majority of users of the language would be included. Corpus-based grammar is the usual approach followed by British linguists, and a similar procedure was characteristic of the anthropological approach in America. Distinct from this is a view, developed over the last ten years, which is at once more theoretical, logical and mathematical in its expression. The movement derives most of its stimulus from the kind of analysis now known as transformative-generative grammar, of which there are now many distinct kinds.[12] Basically the aim is to produce models or theoretical frameworks to account for linguistic data, a grammar being not simply a description of speech forms, but rather a device for generating all the grammatical sentences of a language and only these, using clearly defined procedures called rules. A grammar thus shows how grammatical sentences come to be, and therefore their structure.

This approach is primarily concerned with theoretical equations of symbols and the ordering of rules to produce the simplest model of a language, and it is naturally a more complex approach than the descriptivism of the anthropologists. This is offset, it is claimed, by a corresponding reduction in the amount of information and classification one needs to use to describe a language adequately: the compression brings greater economy and the logic greater generality. The optimism is probably well founded; grammars of the future are going to be grateful for the clarification of the formal organization of language that transformational grammar has provided. But, at the present stage of study, the techniques are still largely theoretical, by no means the totality of language data has been satisfactorily accounted for, and many linguists have raised objections which have not as yet been finally settled—difficulties to do with the way rules are ordered and with the definition of crucial terms like "simplicity" and "grammatical". The arguments pro and con still continue amongst those linguists who have the mathematical and logical knowledge to be able to follow. The controversial and incomplete state of this modern approach therefore precludes its consideration as the basis of the present chapter,

[12] For an introduction, see Bibliography under Bach.

which will be restricted to general considerations of a more familiar nature.[13]

As the anthropological view suggests, grammar as description aims at providing an exhaustive inventory and classification of all the forms and structures of a given language, presented in the form of descriptive statements, upon which different kind of rules can then be based (depending on the purpose of the grammar). A description is based on an examination of the speech habits of as many native speakers as can be subjected to analysis: the practical limitations are of the linguist's time and money only. It is an activity which the linguist must carry out before he can hope to make reliable generalized statements about a language.[14] This is but logical. Although the linguist ultimately hopes to make statements about the meaning of linguistic forms, he cannot do so until he has first described their total usage and range of effect, which demands a comprehensive formal description—sound leads to sense. Again, a description is prerequiste for the drawing up of school textbooks; it is wrong to make recommendations without knowing that what one is recommending is valid (that is, used) —unfortunately, it happens all too often. A vague impressionism, based on what the teacher *thinks* is used, or on what he thinks ought to be, ultimately produces only confusion. Prescriptions about usage and grammatical rules must be based on facts, but facts only come from descriptive surveys, which minimize the subjective element implicit in the linguist's personal views.

What kind of descriptive survey should the linguist carry out? Here there are three possibilities. It can be a purely synchronic description of the present-day state of the language; it can be a purely diachronic description of the history of the language; or it can be a mixture of both. No one kind is absolutely any more important than another; a description can only be judged by what it sets out to do. But in a modern context of linguistic study or in the practical demands of the teaching

[13] The two views are not totally incompatible, of course, and many linguists engaged in corpus-based description are finding the suggestions of the transformationalists highly useful. Moreover, it must not be thought that the anthropological view is itself without controversy.

[14] "The first business of the linguist is description". (P. L. Garvin.)

situation, historically orientated grammars are of no use at all.[15] One does not need a knowledge of Old English, for example, to understand how modern English works. Diachronic considerations provide confusing and irrelevant information in a grammar purporting to be of modern English. Unfortunately, most of the major grammatical handbooks available to date and many school textbooks incorporate this historical bias.

A second objection to most of the traditional handbooks is one of inadequacy, in various degrees: there is a tendency, particularly marked in the smaller textbooks, to restrict the amount of actual data considered to more formal kinds of written language. Certainly there is little attempt made to cover the more informal styles of spoken English, which constitute a statistical norm of usage; nor is there any systematic observation of stylistic ranges of usage, that would form a central part of any linguistically-orientated survey. The result is a distorted view of the proportions and function of language forms; one gets the impression that the language described in the grammar books is normal when in actual fact it is a specialized variety.

The marked ignorance of linguistic principles is evidenced in three further respects. There is a tendency to identify English grammar with statements based largely or completely on written data, only passing reference being made to speech forms. This, of course, is a reversal of linguistic priorities: a realistic linguistic description would make speech the initial focus of attention. Secondly, there is the attempt by many textbook authors to force English into the descriptive mould of another language, usually Latin, the result being misrepresentation and confusion. And finally, there is the impressionistic basis of many of the teaching grammars: statements are based on the author's intuition with little explicit reference to other usages, and are consequently misleading in the generality attributed to them.

If the majority of descriptive works on the subject of English grammar (the language on which most has been done) are inadequate, then, what is to replace them? Modern linguistics is providing an answer, in the form of methodically produced

[15] We have already seen (pp. 39, 58 above) how the most useful diachronic work requires a synchronic description to precede it.

synchronic surveys of all the kinds of English used today. When this has been done, teachers will be able to select their information to teach in class, knowing it to be reliable: better textbooks and language laboratory courses will be written, and impressionistic statements about "how language works" will have a body of data against which they can be assessed. The reorientation takes time, of course, but results are slowly appearing.[16]

It is not possible in this short section to give any detailed study of how a grammatical analysis is carried out;[17] rather the aim is to characterize the main focus-points of the grammarian's attention. Grammar arises as a result of the serial nature of language; it deals with one kind of restriction in pattern that comes from stringing words together into sequences that make sense (sentences). A parade in the street is a unified visual impression: though one can focus the attention on first one part of the parade, then another, it is still possible to take in the whole picture simultaneously. But this simultaneity is not possible in language. As soon as one wants to describe what one has seen, then it is necessary to select words from one's vocabulary and put them into grammatical structures to express the relationships between the words. Language selects linguistic forms, then it orders them: grammar studies the way such forms are ordered. This is done, in the first analysis, independently of the meaning these forms might have—considerations of meaning are normally a later concern. A grammarian who wants to find out what classes of words a language has, for example, or what characteristic structures it uses, will do so regardless of any criterion of meaning. When, having done this, he wants to frame a definition to account for what he has described, only grammatical factors should be included. Meaning-based definitions, such as "The noun is the name of a person, place or thing", or "The sentence expresses a complete thought", are of little value for two reasons: they are ambiguous in their vague

---

[16] In Britain, textbooks are already appearing along these lines, cf. Bibliography under Strang; but the main source of information is going to be the descriptive surveys being carried on at English language centres, in particular the Survey of English Usage at University College, London.

[17] For examples, see Bibliography under Quirk (Ch. XI), Bach, Fries, Halliday, Robins and others.

phraseology (what does one mean by "thing" or "complete"?) which to clarify requires further definition again; and, as grammatical definitions, they say nothing at all about grammar! The foreign learner wants to know how a word or phrase is used, as well as what it means.

Modern linguistic study of the grammar of languages is therefore primarily formal. The linguist looks through a corpus of data for the sequential patterns that express relationships between lexical items, and then describes these as consistently and simply as possible using a grammatical metalanguage. His concern is not "applied": the description is carried on regardless of what practical value his information might have, or at what educational level it might be used. Ultimately, it covers all aspects of relationships, the more subtle stylistic nuances in grammar as well as the more obvious word-classes and sentence structures. The general orientation of grammatical study is largely the result of seeing language as a structure; that is, as an entity composed of discrete phonetic elements which combine in various ways to form more complex units usually called words, which in turn function sequentially to form the major formal units, known as sentences. This articulated approach is in sharp contrast to the older methods, which studied isolated elements of language (for example, a vowel, an accent, or an inflection) along the time scale with no regard for the function of these items in the total structure of the language. Such an approach, it is now realized, was inadequate and accounted for only part of the meaning of a form. Now it is seen that the place a linguistic form has in a structure is the essential guide to its rôle or function in the language; and function is an important part of the total meaning of any form or group of forms.

The main purpose of grammar is thus to describe the way words systematically function in structures, and what the defining features of such structures are. It does not study words as such, for this is lexis, the study of items of vocabulary. It traditionally includes morphology, the study of the internal structure of words; and syntax, the study of the external relationships of words, the way they combine into phrases, clauses and sentences. It will be noticed that the different kinds of pattern isolated here form a hierarchical relationship. At one end of the scale there are sentences, which are defined by their formal independence of any other utterance—they can exist on their own as an utterance, in a way which (say) "there will be a" cannot. A sentence also corresponds fairly closely to what the linguistically naïve native speaker would say was a "complete" expression. Within a maximal sentence, one can then describe the different kinds of clauses and phrases; within these, one finds words, and words themselves can be described in terms of smaller units (called "morphemes") which are studied by morphology. This ordering of the major patterns (for English) is but one possible systematic analytic procedure: other kinds of grammatical model provide alternatives.

Finally, it is important to remember that the word "grammatical" is an uncertain concept in modern study. When is a sentence grammatical, when is it not? Often, it is difficult to say. It is sometimes difficult for a native speaker to be sure, when pressed, if a construction is grammatically normal or not. Such examples of linguistic indeterminacy at the present time would be the confusion in the use of "I will" and "I shall", the problem of "It is me" or "It is I", whether it is possible to say "this house has been being built by me", "the data is very interesting", "the man who I was talking to", and so on. The language is in a state of change, with a newer form trying to oust the old, and it might take years before a settled state is reached. These examples are less surely grammatical, in the sense that one cannot make a definite "yes-no" decision about either usage. It is not simply a case of "It is me" being right and the other wrong: style, context, personal factors all have to be taken into account. But such examples are relatively few, and there is a clear sense in which "grammatical" can be unambiguously used. There would be no hesitation in accepting "The cat sat on the mat" as grammatical, and rejecting "cat the on sat mat the", for example. Finally, the native speaker's feeling about what is and what is not grammatical is very often suspect, as he tends to generalize personal decisions; which is why the linguist prefers to examine a large number of people in many situations—preferably without their realizing it, so that they are as natural in their language as possible. After such a large survey has been made, it would then be possible to define "grammatical" as what conformed to statistically determined norms in the corpus, that is, what was acceptable. Certain sequences of forms would then be allowed as "in" the language; others would be rejected as not.

The grammarian studies sentences; the lexicologist studies words.[18] But the grammarian must also study words to a certain extent because they are the raw material for sentences. What is the difference in their points of view, therefore? The grammarian looks at words to set up a series of word-classes (or parts of speech) to account for regular formal and functional correspondences in word usage in his data. Thus a noun can be defined as a separate word-class, not on semantic grounds, but because it patterns in a certain way with other words around it, and because it may have a definable morphological structure (for example, all words ending in "-ence" or "-tion" are nouns). The label "noun", of course, is no more than a grammatically convenient shorthand: it sums up the characteristics of many words which regularly function in approximately the same way. Similarly, with any other word-classes one sets up for English, one studies the formal characteristics and distribution of each, and reaches a grammatical definition.

Following on from this approach, many grammarians have then divided English words into two types which work in quite distinct ways: grammatical words and lexical words. Lexical words are the "main" words of a language. In the case of English they are the nouns, verbs, adjectives and adverbs, which carry the major part of the meaning of any utterance. Grammatical words (often called "form" words or "function" words) communicate information about what relationships exist between the lexical words, what connection they have to each other; they have less positive meaning, though they are never, of course, completely meaningless. To bring out the distinction, the sentence "The cat sat quietly on a red mat" can be divided along these lines into the two groups: "Cat, sat, quietly, red, mat" are the lexical words; "the, on, a" are the grammatical words. Sometimes the division is difficult to make so clearly, but on the whole it is useful, as the function of the two kinds of words is usually quite distinct. Lexical words are often called "open-class" words; the others "closed-class", because they

---

[18] To be distinguished from lexicography, the art of dictionary-making.

function in sets or systems of words, whose members are finite in number. It is easy to count all the prepositions, or pronouns in English, for example, but impossible to count all the nouns or verbs. Finally, grammatical words are the more stable in language: nouns may come and verbs may go, but the definite article and personal pronouns rarely change their form.

LEXIS

This is the grammarian's interest in words. What kind of information is left, then, for the lexicologist? In studying the level of formal organization in language, there would seem to be a stage after which grammatical techniques can at present provide no new information about linguistic forms, but there are still things left to say about them. The theory of lexis, in fact, is a relatively recent addition to linguistic theory: it was set up to account for those aspects of linguistic form which grammar cannot handle. It asks such questions as, How is vocabulary organized? What kinds of restrictions do items of vocabulary exercise upon each other? What is the tendency of one lexical item to "go with" another? On the one hand, you get phrases which are relatively fixed, such as "spick and—", "hale and—", "eke—", where only one item can occur in the blank space; on the other hand there are less fixed patterns, such as "wipe your feet on the —", or "it was an auspicious—", where it is possible to have alternatives, though some are much more likely than others. At the other end of the scale, it is impossible to say what would fill the space in "the—" or "I saw—" without a detailed knowledge of context. Words which go together in definable combinations are said to *collocate*. Lexical collocation is the likelihood that any particular lexical item will occur in the immediate environment of any other. It thus predicts how likely it is for any lexical items to co-occur, or whether it is possible that they could ever co-occur. Such information is far outside the present stage of grammatical study. It is still formal information; one does not require a knowledge of the meaning of any of the above examples to discover their collocability. It is useful information, also, because it clarifies many dark linguistic corners, such as the complexities involved in the workings of idioms, metaphors, clichés, and symbolism. It is also difficult information to obtain, as a description, such as the one being carried out at Edinburgh, must cover many millions of words, to cover the full range of collocational possibilities for any one item.

One of the implications of collocational study is particularly important. If the meaning of a word is partly determined by the environment in which it can occur, as was suggested in relation to grammar, then collocations are an essential part of any word's total meaning. As Firth said, "One of the meanings of 'night' is its collocability with 'dark' ". One of the meanings of "jam" is that it occurs in an environment where words like "traffic" come, the other is that it is found with words such as "bread". The dictionaries at the moment do not provide this kind of information, of course; they are more concerned with semantic relationships, what words mean rather than how they go together.

But if it is the case that collocations play a part in the total meaning of a word, then the big question arises, Is it ever possible to have perfect synonymity? Interpretative factors aside, it would seem to be most improbable, because no two words are likely to have exactly the same range of collocations; there will always be some potential difference to separate them, possibly realized as an "overtone" or something that it is difficult to put the finger on. "Words are very seldom exactly synonymous" (Johnson). "Change the structure of the sentence; substitute one synonym for another; and the whole effect is destroyed" (Macaulay). In practice, we get by by accepting a certain percentage of common meaning as sufficient for synonymity; but people more sensitive to language, such as poets or interpreters, find the problem very real.[19]

Grammar and lexis, then, study jointly the formal organization of language. They examine certain types of restriction that occur, ignoring others. Thus they would not include phonetic restrictions, orthographic restrictions ("spelling rules") or semantic restrictions (contradictions and nonsense) as part of their study. A description of the grammar and lexis is the central part of a linguistic statement: their study can be an aid to the native speaker, by fostering an awareness of the resources

[19] Cf. below, p. 104.

of his own language and also suggesting where greater individual fluency might lie; they make up the largest part of an English-teaching course, either by teachers or by machines; and they form the main component of machine translation.[20] Only after one has understood what grammar and lexis have to say about a language can one be certain of the validity of a semantic statement.

[20] Cf. below, p. 108.

SEMANTICS

THE RELATIONSHIP BETWEEN WORDS AND THINGS

The problem of meaning has exercised a fascination from Classical times, but the interest has brought problems, not least being what exactly the term "meaning" means. One of the aims of Ogden and Richards' classic book was to sort out the maze of confusion that surrounds present-day usage: they listed and analysed over twenty meanings of the term. Although at the moment semantics (which we might temporarily gloss as the study or science of meaning) is not in the forefront of most modern linguists' attentions, this is not for any lack of interest or inherent defect in the subject. The reason lies in modern methods of approaching language as a whole (that is, including meaning). The present concern, as we have seen, is with formal descriptions of languages, or, more recently, with a more abstract formulation of linguistic rules; but both views concur that a study of sound is necessary before one can go on to study sense, what the sound means. A major criticism of traditional methods, of course, was that they often reversed the procedure, and began with definitions of important terms based solely on meaning, with no formal support at all—such a procedure only led to vagueness and ambiguity.

Linguists, then, have not ignored semantics, as the bibliography indicates. But much of their time has been taken up with clearing ancient views away in preparation for new, trying to jettison old, inadequate techniques, built for different ends, and trying to delimit the boundaries of the subject from such disciplines as philosophy, which would seem, on the face of it, to be much interested in semantics. It is easier to understand what is involved in meaning if one begins with a few misconceptions, so some reference to these old views will now be made.

It has always been a common misconception to say that words *are* what they refer to, that they are concrete entities. It is a feature of primitive belief in the power of words, but is to be found, unfortunately too frequently, in modern society as well. Take this remark by Aldous Huxley's character Old Rowley in his novel *Crome Yellow*: "Look at them, sir," pointing to swine wallowing in the mud, "Rightly is they called 'pigs'". He blamed the word for the feelings the actual beasts aroused in him.[1] The identification of words and things is characteristic of sorcery, word-magic, and the like, where words are considered powerful, influencers of fortune and so on.[2] And in our own society, there is a definite tendency to view words as good, evil, dangerous or dirty. The fallacy lies simply in the fact that there is no necessary relationship between the word and what it refers to. A word "is" evil only by virtue of the connotations it holds for us individually, that is, its mental associations, which derive from our knowledge of the things or situations themselves, which may be evil. This is easily proved, for what may be a wicked word to one person may be quite inoffensive to another. It is amusing to consider, for example, that not so long ago it was considered positively obscene in certain circles to use the word "legs" at all; polite conversation might refer to the relevant part of a table as "table-limbs". Every language has classes of words which have restrictions on their usage: the occupational restriction of scientific jargon, for example. "Taboo-words" are also restricted, but socially or morally so—thus, obscenity, blasphemy, insulting language (in some social contexts, for example, "nigger", "fascist"), can all be tabooed on occasion. And closely connected are the many euphemisms, as when an undertaker is called a mortician, who deals with people who "pass on".[3]

Speech, then, cannot organize things in the outside world. It can organize thought, however, as we shall see; thought exists in people, and it is they who organize things. To miss out the

[1] Cf. Quirk, *The Use of English*, p. 47.
[2] See below, Chapter IX.
[3] Cf. below, p. 123.

middle of the progression, by saying that names and things are identical, is wrong. A further misconception, following from this, is that meanings themselves are things; that when we communicate a meaning we are invisibly tossing something from speaker to hearer. This again is a fallacy, arising from an ambiguity in usage, so that when one hears "What is the meaning of so-and-so?" one assumes that the meaning is something concrete corresponding to the word. But, as will be seen, there is nothing concrete about meaning at all; meaning is a relationship of a kind, a convenient way of summing up a situation.

What led to the development of modern semantic theories? A particular stimulus was the intense interest in words shown by Romanticists of the eighteenth and nineteenth centuries. Much of the poetry and prose of that time displays a fascination in the use of words, their evocation, history and influence.[4] During the nineteenth century, this logophilia crystallized into a largely historical study of meaning (in view of the climate of the times),[5] which was then seen as an aspect of grammar and called first *semasiology*, later (after Bréal) semantics. A series of publications led to the first great synthesis of the subject, by G. Stern in 1931.[6] More recently, the influence of De Saussurian ideas about meaning, in particular his concept of the linguistic "sign", have become apparent, albeit modified, in the different structuralist schools, and the result has been a structural semantics, in which descriptive synchronic work is carried on into semantic fields, the structure of vocabulary and also stylistics —"every major problem of semantics has stylistic implications."[7]

Study has begun with reference to particular languages, and usually particular groups of words in different languages; but there have been some more general issues raised, especially that of the influence language has on thinking and thinking-processes.[8] The present mathematical leaning of linguistics is

[4] For example, Balzac in 1832 wrote: "Quel beau livre ne composerait-on pas en racontant la vie et les aventures d'un mot."
[5] Cf. Chapter III.
[6] G. Stern, *Meaning and Change of Meaning* (Gothenberg, 1931). See also M. Bréal, *Essai de sémantique* (Paris, 1897).
[7] See Bibliography under Ullmann, p. 9; cf. also, Lyons, *op. cit.*
[8] Cf. Bibliography under Whorf, and below, pp. 106-8.

evidenced in semantics too, in particular in relation to the requirements of computer programming for machine translation. Problems of synonymity, ambiguity, translation of any kind, paraphrase, and so on, are all areas in which semantics has found itself useful—at times essential. And finally, there is that special brand of semantics which interests the philosopher more than the linguist. Here, there are two branches involved: work concerned with what might be briefly called the "theory of signs", overlapping with symbolic logic; and work dealing with obscurity in language, and means of correcting it. The sources for views and information about both aspects are given below.[9]

It has already been pointed out that in an act of communication we do not communicate thoughts or ideas, but physical signals. Nor do we communicate words or sentences, because these are grammatical labels, part of a metalanguage which aims to describe these signals of various kinds. And if we say that "messages" are transmitted, this is only on the understanding that there is an earlier stage in which we say that messages are themselves composed of one or more signals. Signals have usually been called *signs* in communication discussion. The word has had a controversial history, competing with *symbol*,[10] *token*, and many others for referring to the function of what is actually transmitted.[11] In view of the essential part signs play in language, some discussion and clarification of their scope is important.

Signs point to something else other than themselves; their meaning is not self-contained. Physical events, out of which signs are made, are not signs *per se*, but only become so when given a function as a sign by human beings, who conventionally agree to interpret it in a given way. A railway signal is of scenic value only until extra meaning is attached to it by a convention;

[9] On the former, see Bibliography under Morris, De Saussure, Fodor and Katz; on the latter, Korzybski, Hayakawa, and logical positivist views, cf. Chapter XII.

[10] "Symbol" is best restricted to a sign which people are agreed represents or has some obvious connection with a concept because of its associations or analogous qualities, such as the coloured smoke at papal elections, or the symbols used in the liturgy (vestments, etc.).

[11] The form of signs in transmission is mainly the concern of the communication engineer.

and noise remains mere noise without an arbitrary link with something beyond itself. This definition of a sign excludes the "natural" cases, where Nature provides one phenomenon as an indicator of another, as when clouds foretell rain. The sign in communication theory requires human interference before it is seen as such. Signs are arbitrary: there is no necessary connection between a sign and what it points to. There are, of course, cases where there are signs which have such a close resemblance to their referents that they might almost be considered as natural representations (symbols) of the object, but the conventional element is always present: such *iconic* signs would include maps, photographs, and ideographic (picture) alphabets, for example; also, some of the more obviously onomatopoeic words, "hiccough", "murmur", "sniff", and so on. But this is just a question of different degrees of detail in correspondence; language has no naturalistic basis, and codes of any kind are, by definition, conventionally constructed.

As seen in relation to language, the conventional nature of signs implies two things: first, that they are deliberately used; and second, that they have a systematic function—a sign standing for an object regularly stands for that object, and contrasts with other signs which do not. Signs may affect one or more of the senses at the same time: speech—sound, writing—sight, braille—touch, much of (say) the liturgy or a television programme—both sight and sound. Further, it is not a necessary characteristic of signs that they should be translatable into other signs, but problems of communication are alleviated if they can: synonymity and long-distance communication would be impossible without this ability. Any code implies translatability. Finally, it is useful to draw a distinction between *sign-types* and *sign-tokens*. A sign-type is a universal, the existence of a sign apart from its use on any one occasion; it is not a physical event, but corresponds to and would be included by our earlier definition of *langue*. A sign-token, on the other hand, is the physical fact of a sign-type used on a particular occasion, either in speech, writing, gesture, or anything else; a sign-event, corresponding to *parole*. It should also be pointed out that there is no theoretical limit to the overall length of utterance that one calls a sign: it is a shorthand term for an acoustic event (in speech) which signifies something apart from itself; and nothing in this definition requires that it should be limited to words alone. A sign could be a phrase or a sentence.

Signs point to or stand for something not themselves. A relationship is thus established, S —— R, where S is a sign and R is a referent ("what is referred to", or designatum). This two-way or dyadic conception of meaning is an advance on the primitive view outlined above, that words are things. It is implied in the dualism of Saussure, and also in mechanistic linguistic thinking. It assumes that there is a direct relationship existing between sign and referent, the meaning of the sign being determinable by observation of environment and behaviour. A behavioural definition of the meaning of a linguistic form is given in Bloomfield as "the situation in which the speaker utters it and the response which is called forth in the hearer".[12]

Now it is relatively easy to demonstrate that a purely behavioural account of meaning, in terms of observed stimulus and response, is inadequate. Linguistic meaning can exist in many instances where referents are not observable in this way. One need only consider abstract phenomena, or displaced speech (talk about things or events not present) to show that there are kinds of meaningful language to which behavioural criteria cannot apply.[13] Secondly, there is the fact of connotation. Connotations are those overtones, associations or interpretations which a sign has that are due to personal feelings or impressions as opposed to the conventional, impersonal "dictionary" meaning of the sign, which is normally called the denotation. They form an essential part of the potential meaning of language on any specific occasion. But it is not a necessary condition of the existence of connotation that it should be accompanied by observable behaviour. For example, you might never have noticed that what you said caused someone pain or joy because he did not show it. Any behavioural definition of meaning, however, is committed to leaving out such information, and hence is again inadequate.

The facts of connotation and observationally-determined denotation are not opposed or mutually exclusive, of course,

---

[12] *Language*, p. 139: the summary is "speaker's situation → speech → hearer's response".

[13] Cf. also, p. 178 below.

and a good semantic theory must cope with both.[14] But the behavioural approach does not allow for the relevance of a mental or psychological element in meaning. There is also a doubt as to the theory's practicability, in view of the vast amount of observation that would be required to determine any meaning conclusively and fully. But it is at least an advance on more primitive thinking, in that two components of the meaning situation are now isolated: sign and referent. These two are essential, an impression one would gain from the literature on the subject, where they occur time and again under various terminologies: expression/content, vehicle/tenor, signifiant/ signifié, name/sense, and the τὸ σήμαινον/τὸ σημαινόμενον of the Stoics. But the simple opposition, as the preceding paragraph implied, does not tell the whole story; it remains inadequate until a third point is brought into the discussion.

Neither signs nor language exist in a world of their own—they are used; and any theory of meaning must allow for the permanent presence of the users. A sign is *given* meaning, by being used in relation to a referent. It is, of course, equally possible for a referent to bring to mind a sign ("What do you call the name of...?"), but here again, the metaphor is "bring *to mind*". This exemplifies what Ullmann has called the "reciprocal and reversible relationship" between name and thing: the sign can "call up" its referent or one of its referents (in the case of polysemia), and a referent can "call up" one of a number of near synonyms—unless, of course, either sign or referent is completely outside one's own experience. But the point is, that such a relationship would be impossible without a human being to bridge the gap. There is therefore no direct relationship between sign and referent, but an indirect one, via a third point that one could call mind, memory-store, personal-association, thought, reference (after Ogden and Richards), or sense (after Ullmann). This triadic conception of meaning (referential meaning) is summed up in characteristic form by a triangle with no base, as shown on the next page.[15]

Meaning, on this account, totally resides in the mind of the individual, and the referential theory thus takes its place at the

---

[14] Cf. Bibliography under Lyons, Chapter I.
[15] Cf. *The Meaning of Meaning*, Chapter I.

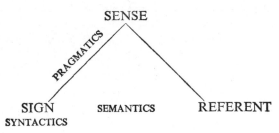

SIGN   SEMANTICS   REFERENT
SYNTACTICS

opposite end of the scale to the mechanistic approach discussed
above. It has been justifiably criticized for its extreme mental-
ism, and there are some further procedural objections which we
will consider below. But at least it does give emphasis to the
crucial rôle of the individual in deciding questions of meaning. The most common use of the word "meaning"—its use as
a near-synonym for "sense"—implies this personal element.
"What does X mean?" is usually synonymous with "What
sense(s) does X have?" And sense, as defined by Ullmann, is
the personal element in meaning, "the information the name
conveys to the hearer" (p. 57). No sign means anything without
the qualification "to whom?".

The fact that there may well be widespread agreement as to
what certain signs mean (especially when referring to observable data) should not obscure this fact, that the individual
has a prominent part to play in determining the meaning.
There is always the backdrop of a person's experience that
governs interpretation and further use. It is this personal element which we have already seen (p. 48) as the ultimate barrier
to communication, most breakdowns in communication being
due not to inefficiency of transmission, but to discrepancies in
interpretation between speaker and hearer. No philosopher
queries the fact of interpretation. Signs mean different things to
different people. It is a cliché that "beauty lies in the eye of the
beholder", but the same point has been made more academically
by the linguist De Saussure: "It is the point of view which
creates the object".

To hedge about "where" this differentiating mechanism lies
is of course to evade the issue: its existence is a necessary
hypothesis to account for the differences in usage which empirical observation brings to light. Nor is this to imply that

individuals need to have some kind of prior thought before they utter signs: the "ghost in the machine" may exist at times, as with careful, premeditated expression, but more frequently it does not. And of course it is not necessary that the linguist should hold any particular psychological theory in maintaining a partially mentalistic position, in just the same way as he is not bound to any one philosophy: questions of meaning can be and should be resolved without reference to extra-linguistic theories.

Some important modifications to the view proposed by Ogden and Richards must still be made in the light of recent thinking. One must now emphasize the reversibility of the relationship, as pointed out by Ullmann; this is an assumption prerequisite for the new field of onomasiology, the study of the meaning-situation by starting with the referent, not, as is more usual, with the sign. One begins with a referent, which could be object or situation, and tries to identify the sign(s) (names or phrases) belonging to it—a procedure utilized in conceptual dictionaries (e.g. Roget), the study of semantic fields in vocabulary, and some dialect study. Secondly, it must not be thought that there is a neat one-to-one relationship existing across the bottom of the triangle: words do not match concepts, nor do sentences necessarily correspond to complete thoughts or "units of meaning". Also there are words which have very little referential meaning at all (e.g. many grammatical forms) and which rather indicate the particular way a referent is to be seen.

A third issue is more important, as it concerns exactly what should be involved in a theory or science of meaning (a semantics). There are three independent uses of the term "meaning" which are relevant here: linguistic meaning, meaning as a kind of logical equivalence, and referential meaning. The first is completely within linguistics; the second, dealing in whether two utterances do or do not mean the same thing, is also relevant; but referential meaning refers primarily to the verification and validating of an utterance in experience, and this, then, is partly an extra-linguistic affair. Linguistic meaning is not reached by studying referents as such, because these belong to the "real world outside", which has nothing whatever to do with linguistics or language. "Reality" is studied by the philosopher, scientist, et al., and is too complex and detailed for the linguist. The meaning of a piece of paper does not lie in its molecular structure; this is linguistically irrelevant. But the triadic conception of meaning admits referents without qualification; there is thus too much information available for the linguist to study.

The semanticist, then (to give him his proper name), only brings referents into his theory of meaning in so far as they are reflected in the language he is studying. He looks at how language parcels out reality—what used to be the aim of many of the now redundant linguistic philosophers. But of course to do this he needs a way of distinguishing between what is the linguistic aspect of referents and what is not; and this requires another, more general, evaluative theory than that proposed by Ogden and Richards. A similar objection can be raised to the mechanistic view. How does one select which behaviour is linguistically significant and which is not in a perceived situation without a more general evaluative theory?

Any theory of meaning needs to strike a balance between the purely mental explanation of meaning and the purely observational, for both are relevant. Denotation is a fairly close approximation to certain characteristics of a generally perceived reality that have been given a name; connotation is the largely individual mental associations of such characteristics or the name (sign) itself. Referential meaning admits too much of reality; behaviourism also, but in addition this finds no place for the mental aspects of meaning. A theory of contextualization is therefore more acceptable to account for meaning as it is grounded more satisfactorily in the language, and has a place for both mental and behavioural kinds of information.

What, then, is context? We have already referred to contextualization in the definition of language in Chapter V as "conventionally patterned noise, contextualized". For present purposes, it is possible to distinguish two kinds of context which determine the meaning of a linguistic sign: they may be called verbal context and context of situation. Both may be "immediate" and "removed". Immediate verbal context is the formal environment in which a given piece of language is embedded—the piece whose meaning one is interested in. This is seen in the technique of citation employed by the Oxford English Dictionary, for example. Contextual considerations begin by determining the formal meaning of a sign in relation

to the different levels of utterance in which it is functioning—
phonological, grammatical and lexical. Each, as we have seen
in Chapter VI, gives a different kind of information; Firth
called each a separate "mode" of meaning. After this, one
proceeds to the semantic mode, which provides denotative information about the sign and is a kind of bridge to the situational context. Removed verbal context, on the other hand,
refers to the meaning a sign has when it is considered in relation
to utterance removed from it in space or time—as when a whole
book needs to be considered before the full meaning of any
particular word or phrase is apparent.

Immediate context of situation[16] is the situation in which the
utterance actually occurs. It therefore includes the immediate
observable antecedents and consequences of the speech act as
well as the personal psychological pressures (observable or not)
that contribute to the total meaning of the sign at that moment.
They may, of course, coincide with, reinforce or contradict to
some extent the information provided by the denotative mode
of meaning. The removed context of situation is the whole
cultural, historical, traditional and psychological background
which may be of relevance in determining nuances, overtones,
and the like. All four are relevant in various degrees in reaching
the total meaning of a sign of any kind.

Taking the word "cross" as an example, one finds that it has
a fairly stable phonological and grammatical meaning, but
when used in, say, a religious handbook on the Passion as
opposed to some non-religious work, it is used with a distinctive
set of lexical collocations ("cross" would tend to collocate with
words like "suffering", "death", etc.), and a highly specific
denotation as well. Study of the removed verbal context would
also add considerably to the significance of the word if one was
aware of further exposition about its meaning later in the book.
The immediate context of situation would be particularly important, as here would enter in the attitudinal variables towards
the word "cross", based on whether one was a Christian or not,
why one was reading, and so on; and the removed context of
situation would also be essential, in determining the overtones
due to the religious background and the traditional position

[16] This phrase has been most widely used in the work of the anthropologist B. Malinowski and that of J. R. Firth.

held by the referent in Christian society, and in one's own world-view. There is thus some overlapping, but each contextual range adds information not obtainable in any other—hence the importance of consulting all four.

The question is often raised, Should linguists be concerned with the meaning of meaning at all? Should they not concentrate on determining the meaning of linguistic items only (as above), and leave such abstract elucidations to the philosopher? It has been said that "the main concern of descriptive linguistics is to make statements of meaning"[17]—that is, not *about* meaning. And this is true, that this is where the descriptive linguist should begin. But sooner or later he will want to proceed to a more general level, to discover the common factor behind all meaning-situations, and there seems no reason why this should be denied him, if he keeps to his priorities, and carries out detailed description first. A definition of meaning would then utilize four variables: signs, context, private meaning (connotation), and the relevant aspects of referents (public meaning, or denotation)—variables distinguished for the purposes of analysis only. And a suggested working definition (one of many possible) could thus be: "meaning is the way people use signs".[18]

Finally, some remarks about the more general implications of the triadic view of meaning, and the relationship between language and logic in particular. The idea behind the referential (or analytical) approach to meaning is to be found in medieval times: *"vox significat mediantibus conceptibus"* (the word signifies through the medium of concepts), and it has exercised a great deal of influence on modern thinking. Until recently, all major semantic theories were based upon it. The triadic relationship was first given a precise formulation by C. Pierce, who suggested that every relationship of this three-way kind necessarily involved meaning. This more general study of the whole field of signs is called *semiotic* (after Locke). It is studied at

---

[17] Firth, "Modes of Meaning", *Essays and Studies* (1951), p. 118.

[18] Cf. L. Antal, *Questions of Meaning* (The Hague, 1963), where meaning is defined as the "rule of sign usage", and the Wittgensteinian operational approach usually summarized (inadequately) as "the meaning of a word is its use". Cf. *Philosophical Investigations*, e.g. p. 150, where words are compared to chess-pieces, and he says "let us say that the meaning of a piece is its rôle in the game" (sc. the language-game).

three overlapping levels (after Morris) which are indicated in the diagram on p. 97 and labelled Semantics, Syntactics and Pragmatics—the totality of interest that a communication analyst would want to study. Syntactics studies signs as such and the relationship which exists between them, a completely formal study; semantics examines the relationship existing between signs and referents; and pragmatics is the branch of semiotic which specifically concerns the user of signs. The latter is the most general and most realistic level of study, as it includes the human being. The others are more artificial, ignoring the users, which only brings one part of the way into the meaning maze, but it is a part particularly complex and much in need of study. Syntactics is the furthest removed, as its totally formal scope makes for treating language as a kind of calculus.[19]

All three levels are described in terms of rules, which are the formal expression of the relationships concerned: needless to say, these rules are not a natural property of language, but are part of the way of talking about language (metalanguage). The rules must not be identified with the real thing. Grammars and dictionaries are not the living language; they always reflect a corpse. Language being in a continual state of flux, all such surveys are necessarily a little or a lot out-of-date; they have to be in a constant state of revision.

Statements describing *langue*, then, and logical statements about language, are necessarily artificial. In particular, language and logic frequently clash, for the simple reason that language is not logical in its form and function; it is often anomalous. A logical analysis of language can never be exhaustive because there is a basic indeterminacy which exists in language that it cannot cope with. It is a commonplace that indecision as to matters of usage exists, and that ambiguity is a living issue. But a logical analysis of language cannot allow itself to be ambiguous or permit indecision. Also it neglects what Firth calls the "implication of utterance",[20] which arises from the interaction of different "modes" of meaning existing at different

---

[19] This is not to be confused with the syntax discussed in relation to grammar, which was a linguistic definition, involving both form and function—a syntactic "mode of meaning".

[20] See "Modes of Meaning", and Firth's report on meaning in *Preliminary Reports for the Seventh Linguistic Congress*, London, 1952.

levels, and the peripheral semantic vagueness which exists and which is, at times, very useful: no one wants to be precise all the time. One remembers Wittgenstein's view of concepts with blurred edges, which he compared to indistinct photographs: "Is it even always an advantage to replace an indistinct picture by a sharp one? Isn't the indistinct one often exactly what we need?"[21]

A logical analysis, then, complements, but does not replace, a descriptive analysis, which would put indeterminacy on the same status as the clear-cut features of language. A logical analysis, also, must be verified by reference to usage, if it is to have any applicability. Two points therefore arise. It is wrong to reverse priorities, and treat usage as if it were dependent on logic, and subservient to it. Logical analyses grew out of a specialist dissatisfaction with ordinary language, not vice versa. Secondly, and following from this, it is wrong to condemn ordinary language for failing to live up to the clarity and consistency which is normally characteristic of logical language: the two usages are formally and functionally independent, and though certain structures may coincide, they are the exceptions. The whole purpose and expression (or logic) of the two languages is different. The "truth" of the conclusions of formal logical rules only holds for the system which produced them: they cannot have a natural language generality, as would apply to the rules produced from analysis of a corpus of data. To take one example, which we will be considering again later: to say that propositions of Subject/Predicate character are a logical norm is a statement which cannot legitimately be generalized to a language as a whole.[22]

SEMANTIC EQUIVALENCE (TRANSLATION)

The discussion of communication earlier implied that because of the number of variables which enter into every situation, perfect communication is not possible. The study of different

[21] *Tractatus*, p. 34. Cf. Bibliography under Ullmann, Chapter V.

[22] See below, p. 187. All work which purports to be description must involve the users, the pragmatic level: a comparison of forms without considering this is a gross distortion: cf. Cherry, Chapter VI, especially pp. 221–2.

kinds of context showed what implications could arise with just two people and one language. Not only are there psychological factors of a personal sort, but of a cultural sort also. Even speaking English, the use of such words as "democracy" and "empire" will produce very different glosses in a conversation between conservative and communist; and different social or religious groups have characteristic words or turns of phrase which other, opposed groups distrust and revile. Of course, the discrepancy is not always noticeable. Two people can be amiably discussing the Mass, and not realizing that they are talking about two very different conceptions of what it is: the opposition could be so extreme as to imply worship and sacrifice to the one, but superstition to the other. In another field, a discussion about the nature of an afterlife is going to succeed only if one continually reinterprets statements in terms of one's own set of values.

If interpersonal communication can be fraught with such difficulties, the magnitude of the international problem of translation, which aims at a universality of sense among whole cultures, will be appreciated. Two Englishmen talking to each other can take so much contextual information for granted; if they know each other well, they can take even more: arguments always go further between people who know something about the other's point of view from past experience. But with two nations, ideologically removed, with different languages, histories and customs—here there is so little in common that problems of communication are greatest of all. There is usually no trouble over concrete objects, or everyday colloquialisms; but as soon as one raises the level of discussion to be translated, then one encounters idioms, abstract words, generic terms, and the like, which carry far-ranging contextual overtones.

A translation is adequate when equivalence is set up between two sets of forms from different languages which are sentences. One does not equate languages word-for-word, not even phrase-for-phrase, as this produces disjointed and unnatural translation; sentence-equivalence is the only satisfactory criterion, and even this has to bear the possibility of removed verbal contextual implications in mind. But how does one assess equivalence? How perfect a knowledge of two cultures and two languages would a person need to have to be able to say conclusively that two utterances mean the same thing in every way? Or, putting the problem another way, how dangerous is it to be satisfied with only partial equivalence? In the nature of things, we must be satisfied with the imperfect and there will always be valid attempts to improve the quality of a translation; but this satisfaction must always be realized as temporary; it should not develop into a complacency, or a naïve assumption that total equivalence is possible, because this can lead to some rude shocks when one finds that comprehension has not been as perfect as one had thought.

It is necessary to be satisfied with language as a communicating medium in translation, because it is all we have; but we should always keep a watchful eye on those areas of language which are most amenable to weakness in equivalence. Such, for example, would be an over-reliance on the possibility of perfect synonyms, which many linguistic and psychological factors are opposed to. Then there is the difficulty of the idiom, which cannot be translated literally but must be taken as a lexical unit demanding an equivalent expression. If there is none, there is only the unsatisfactory alternative of an approximate gloss plus footnote. The same argument applies to imagery—in particular, metaphors and similes: how far can one take liberties with a text so that the meaning of the metaphor is clear though the point of the compared items which constituted the metaphor has been lost? It would seem more legitimate to translate "daily bread" as "daily rice" for the Chinese and "daily fish" for the Eskimo, while saying the *Our Father*; and absolutely pointless to talk about communion as being the "bread of heaven" in such environments. It is a point to be remembered in discussing parables, and suchlike, where the moral is universal, but the form and story may be in terms largely alien to a given culture. The case for adaptionism is clear, and similar arguments can be used in discussing the position of the vernacular in liturgy.[23] One cannot expect to make converts or sell a religion in terms and ceremonies a people cannot understand: no business could succeed on such a principle.

The degree of success of a translation, then, largely depends on the kind of thing one wants to translate: the more general,

[23] Cf. Chapter XI.

abstract, profound, literary, imaginative one's theme, the harder it will be to get exact equivalence in another tongue. There are certain aids: the common source of many important words, in particular where matters of terminology are concerned, makes for something in common among the educated and influential nations, between whom problems of communication are most likely to arise anyway. Thus most European languages have a common heritage in Greek and Latin, with a similar scientific, intellectual and religious background. A similar case could be made out in Arabic and Chinese civilizations. But as soon as it comes to communicating with a different civilization altogether, or with one which has been separated for a long period of time, then difficulties really become noticeable and relatively frequent. It was Hjelmslev who said that the Iron Curtain is also a semantic curtain: meanings, as well as people, find it difficult to pass. And many authors have wondered about a war due to a linguistic mistake, a faulty translation. A study of semantics can help considerably in understanding where the source of a difference or confusion lies, or in suggesting new approaches to an old problem: it is of value in many fields, such as public-relations, industrial management, advertising, literature, politics, and religion.

The commonly held view of the relationship between language, thought and reality has recently been called into question. The usual view is that anyone, regardless of his culture, can talk about certain basic things in his native language, that there are universal concepts, and views of existence which all can grasp if they so wish, each language being sufficiently well-equipped for facilitating cross-cultural discussion on these lines. The ethnolinguistic view, suggested by Sapir and carried much further by B. L. Whorf, opposed this. Its main principle was based on the assumption that people under-estimated the structuring power of language, and that whereas each nation thought it was holding a share in a common world-view, in reality their different languages were imposing different conceptual frameworks, without their noticing it.[24] Whorf has this to say: linguistic analysis has shown "that the background linguistic system (in other words, the grammar) of each language

[24] Cf. Orwellian doublespeak for a similar principle.

is not merely a reproducing instrument for voicing ideas but rather is itself the shaper of ideas".... "We dissect nature along lines laid down by our native languages.... We cut nature up, organize it into concepts, and ascribe significances as we do, largely because we are parties to an agreement to organize it in this way—an agreement that holds throughout our speech community and is codified in the patterns of our language". "This fact is very significant for modern science, for it means that no individual is free to describe nature with absolute impartiality but is constrained to certain modes of interpretation even while he thinks himself most free.... We are thus led to a new principle of relativity, which holds that all observers are not led by the same physical evidence to the same picture of the universe, unless their linguistic backgrounds are similar, or can in some way be calibrated."[25]

There is plenty of evidence for displaying differences in lexical and grammatical structure between languages, of course: the way verbal systems indicate time and activity, the colour system, and kinship terms are popular examples. If accepted, the Sapir-Whorf thesis would play havoc with any system which claimed to embody universal principles, attainable by all, like a world religion. But the thesis can be objected to on a number of counts. First, it is still possible to break out of the chains of our language, even if this is similar, as Kermode put it, to a man trying to get out of a frozen lake: originality is quite possible in language, and most languages are sufficiently flexible to allow shades of meaning between the major structural divisions it possesses—the importance adverbials have in qualifying notions of time in the English verbal system, for example. Second, the fact that language A has a word or group of words which is absent in language B does not mean that B finds it impossible to talk about or refer to the concepts embodied in A's words: both can reach the same end, though with B it will take longer, and devices such as circumlocution, glossing, and word-borrowing must be involved. Thirdly, the thesis implies that all lexical and grammatical structures are of equivalent semantic significance, that each has an important

[25] "Science and Linguistics", *Language, Thought and Reality*, pp. 207–219. Cf. also E. Sapir, "Conceptual Categories in Primitive Languages", *Science*, 74 (1931), p. 578.

part to play in structuring reality. But this is not true. One may take as an example the negligible semantic content of the gender system in most European languages: masculine, feminine and neuter have nothing to do with any conceptual usages. Finally, though it is true that speech, being a patterned response, does produce certain habitual modes of analysing experience, it is not true that intercultural communication and intelligibility is therefore impossible. It may be difficult, but as no two cultures are completely isolated, there are bound to be certain items in common which alleviate the problem—factors of biological, psychological and social importance. The primitive drawings of man turn up in all parts of the world.

To be convincing, Whorf's thesis would have to supplement linguistic evidence with psychological data about cognition: a linguistic analysis is insufficient for psychological conclusions. His ideas have been useful in that they have concentrated attention on a little understood factor of diversification which undoubtedly exists; but it is only one factor among many, and cannot bear the weight of his dramatic conclusions.

Finally, translation should not be confused with the techniques of machine translation, which are not concerned with the meaning of linguistic items, but with ensuring that a programmed set of forms will be turned into an equivalent set of forms in the target language. It is primarily a question of syntactic transformation. The rules for performing the transformations are devised and put into the machines by human beings and, at the other end, it is they who interpret and judge the results. The machine is programmed simply to discover and match equivalences between the formal structure of the two languages involved, though of course it does this at great speed. It is perhaps worth emphasizing that any computer is only as clever as its master, who gives it the relevant information and asks it the right questions.[26]

---

[26] This is a point that needs to be stressed, particularly in view of the recent tendency to overemphasize the place of the computer in research, e.g. in stylometric techniques for determining the disputed authorship of biblical texts. Here is a further field in which linguistic science can provide a valuable perspective, by clarifying stylistic principles and procedures. However, the issues involved are unfortunately too large to be entered into in the present book.

CHAPTER VIII

ON LANGUAGES AND
KINDS OF LANGUAGE

SOME BASIC FACTS

This chapter aims to introduce some facts and general
notions about languages, not already mentioned, and to conclude the discussion, launched in Chapter IV, on the functions
of language. It may come as a surprise to realize that facts
about language are notoriously difficult to come by. Even such
an obvious and apparently simple question as, How many
languages are there? carries its own difficulties. There is no
equally obvious answer. The basic problem is to distinguish
between what exactly the terms "language" and "dialect" refer
to. What characteristics should a language have before it is to
be counted as a separate language and not just a dialect of some
other language? One would not, presumably, wish to classify
Yorkshire dialect and BBC English as different languages,
though there are substantial differences between them, in pronunciation, grammar and vocabulary. On the other hand, such
differences which exist between Norwegian and Swedish are
no greater, and yet it is traditional to take these as
separate languages. Perhaps the most valid criterion for dis-
crimination would be a certain percentage of mutual unintelligibility: total unintelligibility would provide an unambiguous
decision. Put another way, if two tongues have more in common
than they have different, at all levels of language, then they are
dialects of the same language—this is a practical definition,
though it still does not get round the important question of
where one draws dialect boundaries.

But even granted a valid definition of language, as opposed to dialect, one would still have to determine the geographical existence of languages, and this is again not an easy matter. Africa, Asia and both continents of America all have numerous tribes of natives, often numbering only a few hundreds of speakers, sometimes less. One could never be sure that all had been included, and all that *are* known have not yet been sufficiently described. A further problem is the certainty that, whatever the total number of world languages, the figure is decreasing. There are two main reasons for this. The tendency for greater intercommunication and less geographical movement amongst the different tribes is causing less isolation, which is the main cause of languages splitting up into different dialects. The most well-known recent example of a new language is the Pidgin developed in the Far East. Secondly, there is the tendency of certain of the world's languages, for political, economic or other reasons, to dominate smaller groups, and the corresponding desire of small countries to tap the educational storehouse which has accumulated in the language of their larger neighbours. The incentive to benefit intellectually or economically by learning the language of a superior nation is seen frequently, either due to choice or circumstance. Thus many American Indian tribes now speak English; many tribes living in and around the USSR now speak Russian; the Celtic languages have largely been swamped by English—or in the case of Breton, French. Naturally, this procedure tends to allow the smaller language to go out of use: this has happened in our own time to Dalmatian, Cornish and certain Indian languages, for example; it is happening now to Manx, Irish and Scots Gaelic and Welsh, despite brave efforts on the part of nationals to maintain their existence, especially when there is a strongly-felt historical or literary tradition.

While the smaller nations stand to gain by this process from the material point of view, in being able to share in the knowledge of the larger nation, the scholars are not so happy. The linguist, for example, sees the loss of precious data about languages; an irreparable loss, if the language was never written down, for it is the loss of a different way of phrasing thoughts—a matter of concern to the psychologist, archaeologist and anthropologist, as well as to the linguist and the historian. There is a brighter side, however, which may well prove to be of particular importance as a diversifying factor in languages. English, having expanded, and being spoken these days by 250 million people in all parts of the world, has no longer a homogeneous unity. Consequently, different cultures are gradually evolving their own brands of English, some considerably different from the British model: Indian, Nigerian, Australian English, and so on—the differences go deeper than pronunciation, and affect lexis considerably and parts of grammar.

If all these arguments are considered, a conservative estimate of the number of languages in the world might be 2000—a radical view, 4000. Such figures cover a great variety of sizes, of course. Probably the only languages to have more than 50 million speakers are the following (after Malmberg), based on information from the mid-1950's: the figures, in millions, are obviously increasing—Chinese (450), English (250), Hindustani (160), Russian (140), Spanish (110), German (100), Japanese (80), French (75), Malay, Bengali (60), Italian, Portuguese (a conservative estimate) (55), and Arabic (50).[1] It has been estimated that about ·2 per cent of the world's languages are spoken by about two-thirds of its people.

THE USES OF LANGUAGE

Various themes have been discussed in these chapters dealing with the findings of modern linguistics: the principle of patterned likenesses and oppositions, which affects every level of language, and is the basis for the modern view of structure; the continual juxtaposition of the general viewpoint as opposed to the particular; and the importance of seeing language as a social product. Also, there is the persistent conflict which occurs between man and his language. Life indeed came before language, but man finds it difficult to be original and free

---

[1] Here again, figures are very approximate: what is the measure of a person's being able to "speak" a language? The above figure for English corresponds to those for whom English is a first language or "mother-tongue"—and usually, their only language. It excludes perhaps another 100 million people who have a "working" knowledge of the language, but with a very wide range of competence. Cf. Quirk, *The Use of English*, Ch. I.

from "the intolerable wrestle with words" (T. S. Eliot). *Homo sapiens* should not be too facilely identified with *homo loquens*, because there is more to man than his language. Language is rather a tool than a master: "Be not the slave of Words" (Carlyle). If a tool, then, what are the main uses of language? There are many kinds of language-games, as Wittgenstein called them; it is in the interests of linguistics to be able to distinguish these functional differences and correlate them with differences in form. To think of language as one tool for one job is to seriously under-estimate the complexity and flexibility of language.

The different "language-games" it is possible to play in any language depend, of course, on the social functions which require the participation of language in some way. There are three main varieties: style, register and dialect. A particular set of language forms which consistently differentiate themselves from the rest of language by characterizing one kind of interpersonal language-situation is called a *style*. One could therefore go through English describing the various styles it is possible to have, and labelling them according to the situation they characterize: spoken informal conversation between a superior and an inferior, formal prepared speeches, and so on. The number of variables can be many: written language will be a different style from speech; a talk before an audience will be very different from a talk without an audience being present; the manifold styles of literature will depend on matters of disposition, audience, medium, contemporary vogues, etc. All these different kinds of language are styles, in the technical sense: they can all be assessed by a careful description and comparison with an arbitrarily-determined norm, based on statistical evidence.[2]

A style must not be confused with a *register* of language, which is a specialized brand of language existing in a definable social context, but regardless of a particular interpersonal situation, such as the registers of legal, religious or scientific language in English. A style must also not be confused with a *dialect*, which refers to a different dimension of language use much broader than a register. There are two basic kinds of

[2] Cf. N. E. Enkvist, M. Gregory and J. Spencer, *Linguistics and Style* (Oxford, 1964). There are, of course, other, less technical meanings of the term "style" than the one outlined above.

dialect, geographical (regional) or social (*koiné*). The difference is really self-explanatory; a regional dialect is marked by characteristics of grammar, vocabulary and pronunciation (in particular) which make it typical of one part of a country and no other; a social dialect is not bound by regional limitations, but correlates with specific cultural functions, such as status (e.g. public school slang) or education (the type of English taught in schools for foreigners).

Why, then, does language exist? A. Ingraham, in the Swain School lectures of 1903, listed many of the uses of language in this way: to dissipate nervous energy, or release pent-up emotions; to direct motion in others, both men and animals—the imperative function; to set matter in motion (as in charms and incantations); to communicate thoughts and ideas; as a means of expression; as an instrument of thinking; for the purposes of record; and to give delight merely as sound. To these one might add a performative function ("I name this ship...") and a phatic function (the language of polite sociability).[3] Ingraham himself suggests that language is also useful in keeping grammarians busy! It should also be remembered that the types of "thought" or "idea" which language can express are of many kinds: some are relatively sophisticated, or "exotic", as Quirk puts it,[4] others are not—contrast the language one uses in expressing thoughts about science with that used to comment informally about the weather. And there are also the comments of many who have suggested that often language is used to hide thoughts as well as to express them: "The true use of speech is not so much to express our wants as to conceal them." (Goldsmith.) It was Kierkegaard who cynically added that people had no thoughts worth concealing!

We have already mentioned the fact that language is abused as much as it is used, especially when it is criticized for being itself. A major theme of this book has been that no one set of linguistic forms is better or worse than any other. All styles, all registers, all dialects have the same ultimate value in the eyes of the linguist: they are simply differing manifestations of speech, the differences being due to a corresponding diversity of functions. Of course there has to be some kind of standard

[3] Cf. below, p. 171.
[4] *Op. cit.*, p. 35.

language: it is a practical necessity for the purposes of easy communication and teaching. But this norm should not be taken as a rigid authority which has to be followed at all times if one wants to avoid linguistic or social damnation. Unfortunately, such judgements are all too common. They are manifested in statements such as: "You can't say 'It's me'—that's wrong!"; "It's bad English to say 'I only need two'!"; or "You can't end a sentence with a preposition, you know". Linguist after linguist has criticized such views as being self-centred, narrow-minded, vague and unrealistic.[5] They imply notions of a supreme correctness in language, distort the facts of the situation, and add unwelcome pressures to what is already a complex communication situation. There is rarely convincing evidence given for such opinions: Bloomfield found the propounders particularly thick-skinned and unwilling to listen to linguistic arguments.

The reasons supporting a value-judgement are usually quite stereotyped: recourse to a textbook ("It's in Fowler, isn't it?"),[6] aesthetics ("It sounds ugly to say anything else"), logic ("two negatives always make a positive"), analogy (usually with Latin),[7] or writing ("There's a 't' in 'often', so you've got to pronounce it!"). The way such arguments are proposed, however, would suggest a deeper egocentricity: all usage is rejected but the speaker's; other variations are either corrupt or careless. The relevant orientation should be clear from the above pages: textbooks are only guides to language, and should not be confused with the living language itself; aesthetic judgements vary considerably from person to person, and are no basis for supposedly objective linguistic statements; logic and language, we have seen, do not mix; analogical deduction has no foundation, because of the uniqueness of each language's structure; and

[5] See L. Bloomfield, "Secondary and Tertiary Responses to Language", *Language*, 20 (1944), pp. 44–55; J. Warburg, "Notions of Correctness", in Quirk, *The Use of English*; also *The Best-Chosen English* (London, 1961); R. A. Hall, *Linguistics and Your Language* (New York, 1960). For the historical background to the correctness motif, see Chaps. I, II.

[6] H. W. Fowler, *Modern English Usage* (Oxford, 1926).

[7] Cf. Noah Webster, *Dissertations on the English Language* (Boston, 1789), p. 8: "had the English never been acquainted with Greek and Latin, they would never have thought of one half the distinctions and rules which make up our English grammars." Cf. above, p. 82.

writing has no superiority over speech, from which it is derived, and which has a status and principles all its own.

SOME APPLICATIONS

To conclude this section, it is necessary to mention some of the specific applications of linguistics which have not already been discussed: for example, there is the information which semantics can provide in aiding understanding of aphasia, and the relevance of stylistics in determining questions of authorship. Though the study of writing has been largely ignored in the present book, this has been for methodological reasons only, it being a fascinating but logically a secondary sphere of interest for the linguist. We have had to ignore its applications in the teaching of reading, in problems of spelling reform, palaeography (the systematic study of ancient writings), cryptography, and statistical studies in general. Finally there is the rapid and pervasive development of language-learning and teaching techniques. The development of audio-visual aids, in particular the language-laboratory, and the use of the tape-recorder in other fields has helped to give speech its rightful place as the first business of the language teacher. The vast increase in people wanting to learn languages—students, business representatives, missionaries, military and political specialists, and so on, the increasing number of summer-schools in foreign language teaching, the developing textbook industry, and perhaps above all, the heightened place the study of the English language has received in the courses for examination in British schools. There is plenty of work to keep the linguist in business for many years yet, and many applied spheres on which he has not yet focused much of his attention. Religion is one of these.

CHAPTER IX

THE BACKGROUND TO LANGUAGE IN RELIGION

> Take care of the sense, and the sounds
> will take care of themselves.
>
> (Lewis Carroll, *Alice in Wonderland*)

It should now be a truism that everyone uses language, in some shape or form. What might be less obviously a truism is that quite a large proportion of the time dedicated to language-using could have been spent a lot more satisfactorily. We have seen that it is difficult to communicate successfully when the subject-matter gets beyond the concrete; but it would seem pointless to allow difficulties to increase by a lack of attention on our part to the maximal efficiency of language. One can be relatively precise, relatively successful in all communicative activity, if both sides consider the verbal pitfalls and make attempts to avoid them before they begin any form of dialogue. To people who are constantly having to use abstract terms or metaphysical arguments, or even such a simple kind of language as that of the confessional, the need for such care and attention becomes very great.

It will be clear that when one is faced with a religion as formalized and tradition-based as Catholicism, verbal problems multiply at every level. When there is a sacred text to be followed and interpreted, when the words of the Fathers and past Council decisions are so important, when the issue is one of liturgical expression, or when one hears doubts as to whether it is ever possible to talk about a God, then the essential rôle language plays is very evident. The question naturally arises,

Why should this be so? What is the reason for the close relationship that exists between language and religion? One answer must be along the lines that language, being the most flexible tool of communication we have, and the tool most closely tied to the variety of social needs, is naturally going to have the major part to play in that part of the Church's function which is to communicate a religion and to show its members how to communicate with God. Other reasons, based on the indispensability of language in prayer and the formulation of belief and ritual will be discussed later. But there is also an important historical reason, which when examined casts unexpected light on the nature of the relationship between man, his language and the supernatural. The present chapter will examine this reason, before going on to consider the more notable synchronic implications of modern religious linguistic communication.

It is difficult to find a culture which has not evidenced somewhere in its history an awareness of a relationship existing between language and the supernatural. Often this is given explicit expression in literature or legend. We have already seen how one of the most universal of early theories about the origin of language was to ascribe it to a divine source, and examples of suggested inventors can easily be multiplied.[1] To some, speech was undoubtedly the creation of the gods, the power of speech being the gods' gift to man. To others, it was the knowledge of speech (prerequisite for writing) which had been given by the gods. Even if man could speak on his own initiative, it took a god to write down what he said. To the Egyptians, writing was the speech of the gods, and similar ideas exist in other civilizations. The attitude is seen again in the Old Testament. When Moses received the Commandments, the inspired writer had this to say: "And the Lord, when he had ended these words in Mount Sinai, gave to Moses two stone tablets of testimony, written with the finger of God".[2] When people queried the authority of Christ and others, a decisive explanation often given was of the type "for it is written"—an appeal to the

[1] See above, p. 13; also Bibliography under Ogden and Richards (Ch. II), Jespersen (1946) (Ch. IX, X), Ogden; and I. J. Gelb, *A Study of Writing* (Chicago, 1952), pp. 230–5.
[2] Exod. 31. 18. An alternative explanation would be to see here the analogy of the code given to Hammurabi by the sun-god Shamash.

inspired men in the Old Testament; and another name for Scripture is still Holy Writ. In these early days, the higher classes, in particular elders, priests and scribes, were the ones who normally guarded and transmitted writing, or sacred writings, or who used language for special mystical effect—there was usually a special language set aside for sacred ritual. It is only relatively recently that people other than clerics learned how to write. There was thus a natural authority about writing, derived from these various sources, which had overtones of supernatural power. For many centuries the faculty was explicitly reserved for the use of a few.

Now it is probable that such an attitude, of awe and respect tempered with fear, ultimately had its rise in a commonplace natural situation of primitive society. The connection between divinity and language, it has been argued, is evident in the superstitious and mystical ideas about the form and function of language, which affect impressionable natives, and, at another level, children of all ages. The apparently miraculous power of language, for example, is soon appreciated by every child: a cry produces comfort; a simple sequence of sound can make food materialize! Small wonder that creative powers should be attributed to speech. Children look at names with respect; the greatest insult is to make fun of another's name. Words are enquired after, and, when acquired, regarded as valuable. If an object has no name, it is to be feared. These feelings can affect adults too: do they not, when they hear a word, have an image of some kind called up in their minds, yet another form of creativity? Certainly it would have the effect, on the primitive mind, of words apparently controlling objects. Writing was observably omniscient also: it could tell a man things though many miles away from the writer, even about the message-carrier himself. There are many tales of natives stealing an object in a parcel, but delivering the message which accompanied the parcel, only to be found out. The writing had a voice, a life of its own; or maybe a god lived in the letters. From such ideas, that messages "spoke", came many beliefs and theories. Alphabets began to be interpreted mystically, as a proof for the existence of God and other things, and names embodied the power of their owners.[3] One way the true God

3 Cf. below, p. 121.

was to be distinguished from idols was through his voice. He would answer when called upon: they could not (cf. Isa. 46. 7).

The accumulation of all these motifs resulted in images of speech, names, writing, letters and so on being taken as archetypal symbols of divinity, creativity, activity and power. Metaphorical fusions of such concepts are frequent in the literature and legend of many cultures. They occur in both Old and New Testaments, and one image has become part of a fundamental sentence of Christianity: "And the Word was made flesh".

Such matters as the place language held in early Testament times, and the use of language imagery referring to the supernatural in both Hebrew and Greek traditions require a great deal of background research for results of any value. Both literal and spiritual meanings have to be discovered, no easy matter with such a pervasive and permanent symbol. The importance of such research is nowadays well appreciated, however, especially after the encyclicals *Providentissimus Deus* of Leo XIII (1893), *Spiritus Paraclitus* of Benedict XV in 1920, and *Divino Afflante Spiritu* (1943), in which Pope Pius XII emphasized this purpose. "The interpreter must endeavour very carefully, overlooking no light derived from recent research, to determine the personal traits and background of the sacred writer, the age in which he lived, the oral or written sources which he used, and his ways of expressing himself." To begin at the beginning, then, What status did words have in early civilization?

It was only a short step from the appreciation that words were somehow connected with things to the notion that words *were* things, and had a separate existence in reality.[4] The concept of word-souls is seen in places as far apart as Ancient Egypt, the modern Greenlanders, and the pages of Plato. Words were held to embody the nature of things—one of the two positions held by many Classical scholars.[5] But a more important step was to see words as all-powerful, and then to deliberately utilize them as controlling or influencing factors, in both the

---

[4] In this chapter, "words" (or "names") and "things" will be used in place of the more technical "signs" and "referents" introduced in Chapter VII, as most historical work done on this subject talks in this way.

[5] Cf. Chapter I.

divine and human spheres. It is at this stage that religion and anti-religion (including black magic) derive much of their stimulus. Any sphere which deals with the higher functions of thought, the imaginative, the transcendent, the spiritual, necessarily has to contend with both the power and restrictions exercised by words. On the one hand, it is usually impossible to satisfactorily express the deepest and best thoughts, a realization which led Hofmannsthal to give up writing poetry altogether, and which made Faust criticize names as "sound and smoke, befogging a heavenly glow".[6] On the other hand, many poets have concentrated on utilizing the powerful, evocative potential of words to the full. There is magic in the word, a uniqueness which no other word possesses (cf. p. 88), and it is accepted that a rose under any other name would *not* smell as sweet (especially if this other name was "toad", for example). "All words are spiritual" (Whitman). Advertisers and conquerors know the power that exists in words. Napoleon, it is said, preferred newspapers to battalions, Leo XIII warned against the printed matter of the rationalists.[7] Writing and speech are the expression of a nation, also: what better way to remove a nation's influence than to burn its writings? Cortez did this to the Aztecs in 1520, and both Nazis and Allies did it to each other in the Second World War.

Words have always been appreciated as powerful. Runes were originally charms, and the power of a charm or an amulet depended largely on the writing upon it. The more spiritual the subject-matter, the better the charm. One finds this kind of belief in Jewish phylacteries, and in the occasional Christian custom, such as that of fanning a sick person with pages of the Bible, or making him eat paper with a prayer on it. Again, if words control things, then their power could be intensified by saying them over and over again: "The repetitive statement of certain words is believed to produce the reality stated" (Malinowsky).[8] Magic formulas, incantations, rhythmical listing of proper names (a good example is seen in the Old Norse *Edda*), and many other rites exemplify the intensifying power of words,

[6] "Schall und Rauch, umnebelnd Himmelsglut".
[7] *Providentissimus Deus*, 1893.
[8] It was Christ who emphasized that quality not quantity of prayer was what was needed (Matt. 6. 7).

even, at times, word hysteria. There may be both precision and obscurity: one finds the meticulous phraseology and verbal tradition of Sanskrit and Massoretic Hebrew, and the care associated with the Benedictine Rule for celebrating the Divine Office in choir, beside the meaningless verbality of (say) the Avestan hymns, which is itself conducive to mystery and awe. Catholicism, of course, makes use of many kinds of verbal ritual: blessing, antiphonal singing, litanies, invocations, doxologies (greater and lesser), and formulas which can gain sacramental grace, if uttered at the proper time in a proper disposition. Magic (white and black) displays many similar forms. Formulas can be used either to keep evil away or to ask it to come—as Marlowe's Doctor Faustus. Devils can be controlled by language, as can physical matter. Christ casts out spirits "with a word" (Matt. 8. 16), and false exorcists attempt to use Jesus' name as a spell in Acts 19. 13, following. There are many examples in folklore of forbidden names which, when discovered, break the evil power of their owners—Tom-tit-tot, Vargaluska, Rumpelstilskin.

This mention of words in their function as personal labels, or proper names, introduces a more important and awe-inspiring implication, which Christian writers were to make much use of. Again, children's views approach the situation. Children are often anxious to conceal their own names. They hurt and are hurt by name-calling, even with simple distorting patterns. And many primitives do not like to hear their name used, for a personal name is a unique, supreme attribute, wherein resides the whole of one's being. The Bible has many examples of words or names embodying the personality or power of the utterer—thus Isaac cannot retract his verbal blessing wrongfully given to Jacob (Gen. 27. 37), Yahweh sends his word to act for him (Is. 55. 10, 11), monuments to a name maintain the existence of the owner, and so on.[9] Another (non-biblical) characteristic situation might be if a tribal chief takes the name "life"; then a new word has to be found in the language for "life", so that his name is not used in inauspicious circumstances. Nor is it usual for the names of the departed to be uttered, though this is because of

[9] Cf. A. R. Johnson, *The One and the Many in the Israelite Conception of God* (Cardiff, 1961), for a discussion of the idea of personal extension.

fear, not respect: while a name endures, a dead person does also, and those who utter the name bring the evil of death upon themselves. No wonder, therefore, that so little history is known about primitive tribes—for how can history be written without names? [10]

Logophobia, then, affected everyone, but priests, chiefs and gods in particular. If the name involved was one's "secret" or "special" name, then, of course, concern was doubled. Many Australian and New Zealand tribes have this habit; and every ancient Egyptian had two names—one for the world, and one for God, which was never divulged. To know a person's secret name was really to have power over him. Only a god could acceptably know people and use their names so freely. In the language of Scripture, God is said to "know" those whom he approves and loves, and to know "by name" those whom he particularly rewards. "I know thee by thy name", said God to Moses; and it was the greatest of all favours for Moses to be told a name for God at all (Ex. 3. 14), though this was hardly a proper name in any usual sense—"I am who am".[11]

Most Hebrew names, until about 400 B.C. onwards, had meanings, either of a theophoric kind (e.g. Nathaniah meant "Yahweh has given") or designating the quality of the bearer (e.g. Delilah, "little one", Azzan, "strong"). They were supposed to represent the character desired by the parents for the children. Others were of a more "occasional" kind, deriving from circumstance of birth (e.g. Manoah, "resting-place", Zerah, "sunrise"), or significant event, as in Gen. 27. 36, "Rightly is his name called Jacob. . . ."[12] A similar concern for names is seen in some cultures when a person died. If his name was X, then all things named X or other people of the same name had to be renamed. Or, if a child died, the next by the same mother would be called by some evil name, to show the death spirit that the child was not worth bothering about. The name was to have the effect of a talisman (e.g. Gareb, "scabious"; Nabal, "fool"). In the Roman levies, too, the authorities took good care to enrol first men with auspicious names

[10] Cf. H. Webster, *Taboo: A Sociological Survey* (London, 1942), pp. 184–7, 299–303.   [11] Cf. below, pp. 124, 128–9.

[12] Cf. L. Köhler, *Hebrew Man*, trans. P. R. Ackroyd (London, 1956), pp. 63–7; and J. Pedersen, *Israel: its life and culture* (London, 1926), I–II, pp. 245–9.

—Victor, Felix, and so on. Christ also was to pay great attention to the renaming of Peter.

This kind of verbomania, which at times modulated easily into superstition, existed pervasively in different degrees of intensity in many cultures and ages. When Adrian VI became Pope, for example, he was persuaded not to retain his own name on the grounds that all Popes who had done so had died in the first year of their reign. Today, the fear of certain words is as strong as ever: [13] euphemisms abound, and there are many who hate to use words referring to sex or death, or who use "mild" forms of God's name as emphasis. It is difficult to find clear-cut reasons for the pervasiveness of linguistic superstition, apart from those already suggested. The permanence of the themes is partly explained by the fossilization of older habitual forms of thought in languages, which in later ages exercised some influence on the user's thinking processes. Every language has characteristic patterns and idioms which in some measure channel the thoughts of the users, usually unconsciously.[14] Thus, the fact that a proper name should be seen as enclosing an individual as well may not be so surprising when one considers the tendency in many languages to use metonymy, where the name of an attribute is substituted for the thing meant; the part is seen as the whole. A head can stand for a man (heads in the crowd), or a crown (when he is king) or a hand (in a vote), and so why not a name? In Daniel, languages "trembled and were afraid" of Nabuchodonosor (5. 19), and in the Apocalypse, "there were killed in the earthquake names of men seven thousand" (11. 13). Again, an accent to many today in Britain is still inseparably associated with status; the way a man speaks is taken as a character indicator (cf. the "voice of authority" in the Lord), and all too often it is assumed that a new accent covers a new man. There are still many traditions and ceremonies which require a change of name to accompany a change of state: women who marry, towns (for example, St Petersburg, Leningrad), kings, popes, and three sacraments are affected (baptism, confirmation, and often holy Orders). Finally a study of English idiom brings out how thoroughly language is perpetuating its own importance in our speech—"hold your breath", "keep your mouth shut", "don't breathe a word", "a

[13] Cf. above, p. 91.   [14] Cf. above, pp. 106, f.

waste of breath", lies "roll off the tongue", and many more. To look closely at the literal meaning of such phrases is to perceive some of the ancient ideas about the power of words.

Of all the words used as proper names, however, one group was always singled out for special emphasis: these were the names connected with the divinity. God's name was never to be spoken carelessly. To use this name, even unintentionally in inauspicious circumstances, was blasphemy. Far more serious, then, was the deliberate misuse: "Thou shalt not take the name of the Lord thy God in vain" (Ex. 20. 7). A similar idea is seen in *Cratylus*, where the debaters worry about using gods' names as etymological examples, and elswhere in Greek mythology. To guard against profanation, the names of Greek gods were carved on stone and sunk in the sea. Herodotus will not name Osiris, and the true names of Allah and Confucius are secret. The Jews out of reverence did not pronounce the divine name as it occurred in the Hebrew (around 6823 times, either on its own, or in combination with other names for God). It was written with four consonants, YHWH (the tetragrammaton), vowel-points not being written in pre-Massoretic Hebrew. In reading, however, the Jews substituted 'Adonai (or 'Elohim). The form "Yahweh" is a scholarly attempt at reconstruction, interpreting its meaning as part of the verb "to be" to give, as Heinisch claims, the title "the One Who Is", an appropriate name to indicate the eternal, self-existent nature of God.[15] Jehovah is a name which has only been traced back to the fourteenth century: it is reached by inserting the vowels of 'Adonai under the Tetragrammaton, and arose from a misreading by Christian scholars of the two sources as one word. It is thus not of Scriptural origin, and the true pronunciation of YHWH is now quite lost.[16]

God's name, then, was "taboo" (a Polynesian word for what is holy and untouchable); it had to be treated with greatest respect. Normally only the high priest would have knowledge of the divine name—hence the many synonyms and circumlocutions when others referred to the deity—and even he would

[15] Cf. footnote sixteen below, and further on p. 128.

[16] For the different names for God used in the Old Testament and their meanings ('el, 'elohim, etc.) see O. Grether, *Name und Wort Gottes im Atten Testament* (1933), P. Heinisch, *Theology of the Old Testament*, trans. W. G. Heldt (The Liturgical Press, 1955), pp. 36–44.

use an equivalent reticence, as he would only whisper the name once, on the Day of Atonement. We bow our heads still at the name "Jesus", and since Gregory X, the zeal of the Dominicans has kept the Holy Name Society very much alive, with four million members in 1959. Josephus the historian tells how only skins of "clean" animals could be used for copies of the sacred Law, and the Talmud was similarly affected: the subject-matter was too sacred. From another point of view, once the billion names of God have been intoned (goes the legend) the world will end, because its *raison d'être* will have ceased to exist. (Recently, someone has wanted to test this, using a prayer-wheel powered by an electric motor!)

A brief examination of such matters in the Old and New Testaments shows clearly that "the Divine is rightly so-called". The authors of Scripture, partly because of the natural tendency of their idiom, partly to meet the demand of historical narra-tive, were careful to label things. Long lists of names (gene-alogies) frequently occur: there is a concern for precision —rivers, mountains, blood relations are all named, and often given additional glosses to minimize ambiguity and increase signification. The pattern occurs again and again: "Therefore the name is called X", "so he called the name of his X, Y". The New Testament is merely telling the story when it says "and the virgin's name was Mary" (I k. 1. 27), but the writer is follow-ing convention in "And they shall call his name Emmanuel, which is, interpreted, 'God be with us' " (Matt. 1. 23). The same pattern is in Genesis: "Thou shalt call his name Ishmael, because..." (16. 11), "Thou shalt be called Abraham, because...." (17. 5). This concern for the signification and justification of names occurs regularly: the urgent "because" appears again in Matt. 1. 21. There is much debate over suitable names,[17] especially as to whether they conform to the will of God: one remembers the discussion in Luke 1 about the name of John the Baptist, and when the angel was sent to change Jacob's name to Israel (Gen. 32. 38). The theme is pervasive: "A good name is better than great riches" (Prov. 22. 1) ... "than precious ointments" (Eccles. 7. 2). The main opposition is between perpetuating the memory of a name, and blotting it out for ever: these are the

---

[17] Cf. above, p. 122.

matters of supreme importance. The Lord threatens to destroy the Israelites by saying he will "abolish their name from under heaven" (Deu. 9. 14). This was the most powerful threat of all. It is much more than metonymy. The blotting out of a name symbolized the *total* obliteration of a person's existence, as if he had never been born.[18] On the other hand, the name which is to be praised for ever, and which is the most permanent could only be God's. "I am who am ... is my name for ever", said God to Moses (Exod. 3. 14).

One of the most frequent verbal patterns to occur in Scripture is "the name of the Lord". From the very beginning, mankind worshipped God, though the name Yahweh seems only to have been revealed in the time of Moses.[19] There are a number of inter-relating attitudes. First, there is God's own command to worship his name (by metonymy, himself). The Lord said to Moses, "And therefore have I raised thee, that I may show my power in thee, and my name be spoken of throughout the earth" (Ex. 9. 16). This then evokes the desire of his people to magnify his name for ever.[20] Many of the Psalms take up this theme: "I will sing praise to your name, Most High" (9. 3);[21] and much later the Gospels display it in a multitude of contexts: "Hallowed be thy name" (Matt. 6. 9), "He who is mighty has done great things to me, and holy is his name" (Lk. 1. 49), "And this is his commandment; that we should believe in the name of his Son Jesus Christ, and love one another" (1 John 3. 23). The echo is compelling. The Lord is symbolized by his name dwelling in a place;[22] remembering his name is a duty to be affirmed at all times: "By night I remember your name, O Lord, and I will keep your law" (Ps. 118. 55). And what is the name worth? Many things, for God has revealed his omnipotence through his name. It can bring a blessing (Num. 6. 27), produce a favour, enlist the power of God (Ps. 53. 3), support a plea —Jeremias asks "for thy name's sake" (14. 21)—and God has promised to stand by the power of his name: "For my name's sake I will remove my wrath far off" (Is. 48. 9). It is associated

[18] Cf. Deut. 25. 6; 2 Kings 18. 18.
[19] Exod. 3. 14; 6. 3. Cf. Gen. 4. 26, 12. 8, 13. 4, etc.
[20] 2 Kings 7. 26; 3 Kings 8. 20; 1 Para. 16. 29, 35, etc.
[21] Cf. also, 7. 18, 33. 4, 74. 1, etc.
[22] Cf. Deut. 16. 2, 6, 11, 15. . . .

with the idea of reward, particularly in the Gospels:[23] "If you ask me anything in my name, I will do it" (John 14. 14). One significance of this is that a little later, Christ goes on to say, "If you ask the Father anything in my name, he will give it to you" (John 16. 23). Such careful juxtaposition of the name of the Father with that of the Son in a similar syntactic structure, especially found in St John, implies that the two names fulfil an identical function. The tradition being what it was, a retrospective view strongly suggests the unity of two persons in one nature. Again, when names were so powerful and individualistic, to say that two persons had one name (even though otherwise distinguished) was to stress an identity very closely indeed. It is seen in the metaphor of the Word, already discussed, and is continually before us in the Sign of the Cross, in the "name" of Father, Son and Holy Ghost.[24] Similarly, such references as John 5. 43, "I have come in the name of my Father" must be interpreted as more than a passing reference, as if someone had put his father's visiting card on the table; it is a much stronger fusion, due entirely to the importance attached to proper names at the time.

A similar kind of linguistic manipulation is seen in the Old Testament. To attempt to describe adequately the many-faceted nature of God required a distortion of the normal forms of language, so that his exceptional nature would be at least hinted at. The word for God in the Hebrew ('elohim) is plural in form, though it normally takes a singular adjective and verb;[25] and it is also possible to interpret such a deliberate pronominal change as in Isa. 6. 8. as a prefiguration of the Trinity: "Whom shall I send, and who shall go for us?" Once again, the elements of oneness and plurality are side by side.[26]

As one might expect, blasphemy was a major sin in the Old Testament, and appreciated as such. The prophets exhort time and again to fear the word of the Lord (Ex. 9. 20) and not to defile God's name.[27] To ignore or condemn the word of the

[23] Cf. Matt. 19. 29; Mk. 9. 40, 13. 13; John 1. 12, etc.
[24] Cf. Matt. 28. 19.
[25] But cf. 1 Kings 17. 26; Jer. 10. 10.
[26] Cf. also Gen. 1. 26–7, 3. 22, 11. 5; one could compare the royal "we" in modern use.
[27] 1 Lev. 18. 21, 19. 12; Deut. 5. 11, 18. 20, etc.

Lord (where "word" is synonymous with "command") had a similar fate—destruction (Num. 15. 31). The order is clear: "fear his glorious and terrible name" (Deut. 28. 58). But in the New Testament, more emphasis is laid on the merciful side of the message, on the happiness and peace the name of the Lord can bring. The justice of God is never forgotten (cf. John 3. 18), but there is less talk of power and destruction than in the Old: "Blessed (happy) is he who comes in the name of the Lord" (Matt. 21. 9). The emphasis has been changed, also, in another, more important way, for on a number of occasions, our Lord expressly declares that mere name-calling is quite inadequate. The "sounding-brass" methods of worship which are frequently alluded to (in relation to the Pharisees, for example) would seem to indicate that large numbers paid only mouth-worship to God (cf. Matt. 6. 17), and called on his name thoughtlessly. The Sermon on the Mount indicates what must accompany the name-calling: "Not everyone who says to me 'Lord, Lord', shall enter the kingdom of heaven; but he who does the will of my Father. . . ." "Many will say to me in that day, 'Lord, Lord, did we not prophesy in thy name and cast out devils in thy name, and work many miracles in thy name?' And then I will declare to them, 'I never knew you' ".[28] Actions, it is clear, speak a more heavenly dialect than words.

With so much emphasis on God's true name and its power, then, it is significant that there is so much secrecy about it in the Old Testament, as opposed to the more personal, human revelation in the New—though even here the "proper" name of God the Father is never given. The angel of the Lord (who is identified with God by the writer)[29] will not give his name. After Jacob has had his name changed to Israel, he naturally asks, "Tell me by what name art thou called? He answered: Why dost thou ask my name?" (Gen. 32. 28).[30] And the Hebrew when God gives his name at the burning bush is ambiguous: "I am who am" is the normal rendering, but "I am who I am" and "I am because I am" are quite possible, as are further renderings if one takes the verb as future or as meaning

[28] Matt. 7. 21–3. Cf. also 15. 8.
[29] Perhaps another example of the extension theory, that the messenger was indistinguishable from his lord, cf. Judges 6. 12 and Johnson, *op. cit.*
[30] Cf. also Judges 13. 18.

"become". When one realizes that the behavioural definition of a name, seen as the summation of its effects, was the normal mode of reference, then the absence of a specific personal title becomes less relevant, of course, for there are many circumlocutions referring to God ("King of Kings", etc.) which indicate his supremacy and glory as far as human language can. "I am the First, and I am the Last" (Isaias 44. 6; 48. 12) is another example, to be echoed later in the Apocalypse, "I am the Alpha and the Omega"[31]—an apotheosis of all things wonderful, if one bears in mind the mystical significance of the alphabet and writing. As a symbol of infinite perfection, this must have been unequalled. Its effect was permanent also: as a Christogram it was frequently used in post-Arian days to reaffirm the true divinity of Christ, and is a common enough figure today. Much of the impression one gets of God in the Old Testament, then, is of majesty, power and vastness; this is often due, it can be argued, to the depersonalizing effect of no-name (because above naming) and formula-reference (praising "the name of the Lord").

There is a definite contrast with the person of God the Son in the New Testament. His name is clearly given and interpreted: Jesus Christ, which means Anointed Saviour; a human form, but with both divine and human function. This was much more readily understandable and lovable. His name is explained, used, died for: Ananias is told how Saul must suffer for the name of Jesus (Acts 9. 16). When Jesus asks Peter who He is, there is no uncertainty about the reply: "Thou art Christ, the Son of the Living God". There is still the magnificence— his name is "above every other name that is named, not only in this world, but also in that which is to come" (Ephes. 1. 21)— but the language of Father and Son, and the name Christ itself are more specific and more pervasive. By the time of St John, it was possible to use "Word" without qualification and without ambiguity to refer to Christ, and in the Apocalypse three important strands of meaning are brought together: "And his name is called the Word of God" (19. 13). What would be the implications of such a statement?

Egyptian history of ideas tells us that the world exists only because Thoth interpreted the will of God in words. All things were made through God; but all things also came into being

[31] 1. 8, 21. 6, 22. 13.

through an act of speech. God and speech thus assume a unity of function. To the Hindus, speech is a manifestation of the creative power of Brahma, who created the earth by uttering the word *bhū* ("be"), and who gave miraculous power to many early words. In Genesis 1, God is represented as creating via speech. Such views gave a god a kind of behavioural description; his meaning lay in the power attributed to him, this power being manifested in his act of utterance—later in the act of using his name. The attribution of the power of naming to the divinity, or to his representative (for example, Adam), we have already seen resulted in an overlapping of the name function with religious significance. In the Pyramid Texts, there is mention of a God Khern, whose name means "word"; and in Christian thought, the central metaphor also became "word". In Hebrew thought, "word" stood for a number of things. In a religious context it primarily referred to the Hebraic prophetic experience of hearing the word or message of the Lord, the communicative activity initiated by the Divinity—Hebrew "dabhar" also denoted "event" or "act". As such, it also denoted the "inspiration" which an individual prophet received,[32] as opposed to the simple "message" in a dream or vision (Gen. 15. 4). In the Old Testament, the metaphor also expressed God's creative power and omnipotence: "By the word of the Lord the heavens were made; by the breath of his mouth all their host" (Ps. 32. 6), "God ... who hast made all things with thy word" (Wis. 9. 1). In particular, the "word" stood for the divine law given to Israel by God through Moses.

The metaphor was to become of central importance in the New Testament via the personification of John 1. 1: "In the beginning was the Word, and the Word was with God; and the Word was God". This is an original idea of John's, as far as one can tell. The nearest one gets to personification in the Hebrew is the metonymy of "the word of God" for God himself, a reverent circumlocution. But it is never given the same independent, unqualified status as it is in John. Nor is there much in traditional Hellenistic ideas to stimulate his usage. The Platonic idea of λόγος, as later expounded by the Stoics, and Philo of Alexandria in particular, could have influenced

---

[32] Cf. Osee 1. 1; Jer. 1. 4, 11; Ezech. 3. 17; "and thou shalt hear the word out of my mouth and shalt tell it them from me".

John, but recent scholarship as well as St Augustine[33] suggests
otherwise. Once again, the personal element in the evangelist's
meaning of "Word" is lacking; the λόγος was an impersonal
force, existing from all eternity, a kind of divine Reason govern-
ing all things, the operating principle of the Universe. It is
inadequate to explain John's use, which seems to be a deliberate
departure from the normal mode of thought. It is notable that
he uses "Word" only in the Prologue in the Fourth Gospel:
after 1. 14, "word" (apart from its referent as "ordinary
speech") refers to the message of Scripture only, the traditional
use, and John refers to Christ using more usual metaphors and
his proper name. This was a more normal treatment, particularly utilizing the "wisdom" theme of the Old Testament: Paul
uses it also in 1 Cor. 1. 30: "Christ Jesus, who has become for
us God-given wisdom, and justice, and sanctification, and re-
demption." In the Acts of the Apostles, and the other gospels,
"word" also carries on the Old Testament meaning of "law",
with the new emphasis of Christ's teaching and the missionary
teaching carried out at his command.[34]

What was the purpose of the metaphor? There are a number
of possible implications. It is primarily a unifying metaphor,
bringing together God, Christ and his message. The λόγος is
God, existing from all eternity. The will of God is manifested
in his word, the divine command issued to Moses. At the same
time, there exists the second person of the Blessed Trinity, who
is also the word, or expression, or "intellectual emanation"
(Aquinas) of the Father: it is to this "word" that John gives
the name "Word"—the λόγος become man, whose purpose is
to affirm and teach the "new" word, or divine command. The
nature of God is realized in Christ; the will of God is realized
in his teaching: "that which" we have heard (concerning the
Word of life) becames "he who" we have heard. Jesus pro-
claims the Gospel (from Old English "godspellian", meaning
"good tidings"), and the Gospel has no meaning apart from
him. People will be reborn to a spiritual life by hearing and
following the word-Word. To disagree with the word is to lead
to blasphemies (against the Word).[35] The juxtaposition occurs
in all contexts: the Word creates, and the word is the product

[33] Cf. *Confessions*, vii, 13.   [34] Cf. Acts 4. 4, 29, 31, etc.
[35] Cf. 1 Tim. 6. 3–5.

of divine activity, requiring action, not just passive acceptance on our part;[36] the divine Word is the source and human words the medium of all expression, hence of all learning and wisdom: *"Car le mot, c'est le Verbe, et le Verbe c'est Dieu".*[37]

The metaphor was thus very effective for displaying the fusion of Christ and his Gospel, and it represented equally well the relationship between the Father and the Son: "... and the Word was God." The third person of the Trinity does not fit in so readily. The Apologists found it difficult to include the Holy Spirit as part of the Word imagery—Irenaeus talks of Wisdom instead. But there is a similar metaphor consistently used in relation to the Holy Spirit; the idea of the living breath, who brings the gift of tongues, the source of wisdom. It should not be difficult to see the major correspondences between the description of the Holy Spirit and those of the other two Persons; and a good case can be made out for seeing in the metaphor a useful image of the Trinity.

Further, language having the central part in our lives that it does, the metaphor of the word finds readier understanding than many others. The sower sows the word, and Acts 12. 24 affirms the metaphor: "But the word of the Lord continued to grow and spread"; and its fruit is more powerful sustenance than ordinary food.[38] The other Old Testament uses are also maintained: the word is inspiration for John (Lk. 3. 2), and a command for us all.[39] Finally, one of the most vivid and relevant uses is to help phrase a serious personal warning about the use of one's own speech, which, as a deliberate activity, has a certain moral value: "But I tell you, that of every idle word men speak, they shall give account on the day of judgement. For by thy words thou wilt be justified, and by thy words thou wilt be condemned" (Matt. 12. 36–7). One is reminded of the Book of Psalms, in which we are told that to take the enemy's side is to "speak as they do" (72. 15). The implications of the metaphor are endless. In the context of the Incarnation, the concept becomes all-embracing, including overtones of activity, life, power, inspiration, authority, service, personal knowledge ... in fact, an aphoristic climax to Christianity: "and the Word was made flesh."

[36] Cf. Mark 4. 13, ff.   [37] V. Hugo, *Les Contemplations*, I, i, 8.
[38] Cf. Deut. 8. 3; Matt. 4. 4.   [39] Cf. Lk. 4. 36, 11. 28.

CHAPTER X

LANGUAGE
AND RELIGIONFUL
CHRISTIANITY

SOME ASPECTS OF THEOPHORIC LANGUAGE

While a knowledge of the historical interrelationships existing between language and religion is important in helping one understand the former's rôle as a means of expression and a source of imagery and symbolism, it is the synchronic aspects of the relationship which are more readily appreciated as of universal relevance. Whatever their origins and development, language and religion exist and interact around us *now*, and operate in the same social milieu, both are the product of society, and exercise a pervasive influence on its activities, which are our activities. And as all social intercourse of any complexity requires the use of some kind of language, the most wide-ranging and flexible communicative tool we possess, religion finds itself continuously coming up against the need for utilizing the potential for linguistic self-expression to the full. The supernatural has to be made available to sensory perception using signs and symbols, and this brings its own problems, many of which will be discussed below. All religious fields, theological, pastoral, liturgical[1] and biblical, need to consider language carefully before they use it, for an adequate realization of their purpose: use without consideration leads to mis-

[1] The pastoral field is given separate consideration elsewhere, cf. D. Crystal, "A liturgical language in a linguistic perspective", *New Blackfriars*, December, 1964.

understandings, misrepresentations, and a multitude of other distortions.

One would have thought that the central function of language in all these fields would have prompted a closer, methodical examination of its form and effects, particularly when the science of linguistics began to produce results; but so far, with a few notable exceptions, studies have continued with little additional interest. The following chapters aim to illustrate some of the ways a knowledge of what language is and how it works can assist a better appreciation of what is involved in the exercise of a religious activity of any kind. Ultimately, much of what is said resolves itself into common sense, and there is no attempt made to blind with technical terminology. Rather the aim is to suggest new ways of considering familiar topics, more in line with the principles and practice of the discipline of linguistics. An apology is made in advance for amateurish theological statements, but when these had to be made, it was for the sake of continuity.

Language has been an integral part of Christianity from the beginning. Originally, the Catholic religion was a verbal message, which came to be written down; first an oral, then a scriptural tradition. This resulted in textual studies of various kinds, and interpretative work deriving from both traditions to produce a verbally-expressed theological and liturgical structure. Since then, two activities have been carried on simultaneously, involving exegesis of statements already made and accepted as the basis of faith: internal clarification, so that the faithful come to understand more fully what their religion means; and external explanation, so that the message can be transmitted to the whole world, and be understood. Both aspects are contained within the same theological framework, however, and objections that are made to the apologetic basis of the one, *mutatis mutandis* apply to the other also. One important question has been raised: whether it is possible to use language to talk about the fundamentals of belief at all. This will be discussed in more detail in Chapter Twelve on logical positivism, but the issues must be introduced here. The main object of attack is, of course, God, but now there is a linguistic perspective to the debate: it is no longer a question of believing in God, but in determining the meaning of statements which refer to a God. If one believes, one makes statements which can be subjected to language analysis, and which correspond in certain important respects to other statements made in the past, either in the Bible, or in Council decisions of doctrine. A linguistic definition of a heretic would be one who made statements which did not tally in this way.[2]

The kinds of question most often heard would take the following forms. How can one use language validly to refer to God at all, a finite tool for an infinite referent? How can one express the inexpressible? And if language has not got the potential for referring to God adequately, how can one legitimately use any religious language? It is not enough to use a kind of analogical language about God, it is argued, or to treat him wholly in anthropomorphic terms; for if we talk about God in words normally designed to cater for human characteristics and activities, then this is to be grossly unrealistic. If, for example, one says that God is merciful, one must mean more than the equivalent human situations in which mercy has been shown. But then how does one define what this "more" is? Is it possible to use language to get at it at all, when every word we utter has a referent which is solidly embedded in a human context? On the other hand, one could conclude, to say that God has a meaning undefinable in human terms is to say that one can never know anything about the true meaning of words used about God, and this is linguistic agnosticism.

This is not the same kind of approach which the logical positivists used, who queried the possibility of verification for religious and other metaphysical statements, but it results in the same conclusion. Language is a social fact, whose meaning lies in human experience; but as God is beyond human experience, one cannot therefore talk about him. This is a dramatic attack, but, luckily for the theist, the conclusion needs drastic modification, as the following paragraphs hope to show.

An important line of argument for the Christian is based on the way a technique of language use is introduced into a society: it is taught. A linguistic ability or habit is always learned; language in any form is not instinctive, and each new

[2] Cf. Bibliography under Ferré: the function of the Bible, in linguistic terms, is "to licence the use of certain linguistic formulae and to ban the use of others" (p. 93).

manifestation of speech or writing requires a teacher, or at least someone to imitate.[3] With no teacher there would be no language. And the most obvious reason why we can legitimately use language to talk about God is because we have been taught to do so, by the prophets, the sacred writers, and above all by Christ himself, who told us what to do with it, how to pray. The source to imitate and understand is clear. What then were the language habits of the early writers, and of Christ himself, when they began to talk about God? In the absence of any systematic description of the style of the Bible, one must be impressionistic, but the answer will be clear, and the above objections found to create merely pseudo-problems.

In the Old Testament, one finds a continual use made of anthropomorphisms, where man's actions or dimensions are ascribed to God or to his angel.[4] God is attributed human functions of every kind apart from vices: there are emotional, intellectual and volitional manifestations; he speaks and acts, shows mercy, pity, anger, and many other qualities. Doubtless the reason for this view lies in a number of tendencies, such as the oral tradition which the sacred writers tapped and the literary forms which were most familiar at the time, or the natural tendency of man to see everything in his own image, which is reflected in his language.[5] But in all such instances, God is never said actually to be human; the activities are ascribed to him usually in an undefined and indefinite way. The anthropomorphic language suggests a point of immediate comparison, so that human understanding can be channelled in the right direction rather than not at all; the comparison is not intended to be complete or precise. God is never given a specific one-to-one correlation with the human condition.

Christ's language in the New Testament is also orientated towards popular understanding. The short and extended similes, the traditional symbols, the Old Testament quotations, the vivid metaphors and parable narratives: this was popular, familiar language used to communicate a body of teaching to a largely uneducated public—which is exactly what one would

---

[3] Cf. above, pp. 69–70.

[4] Cf. Exod. 33. 23; 2 Kings 22. 25.

[5] Cf. Bibliography under Ullmann, Ch. V, for many examples of this anthropomorphic habit in ordinary language.

expect. Christianity is for all; it must therefore be comprehensible to all. Also, there is never any suggestion that because one cannot understand a point of the teaching or because a truth is only partially explained, that one should stop trying to understand or become dissatisfied with what one already has had revealed. Nor is there any point in crying for a linguistic moon by worrying over the inadequacies of ordinary language. "Human language is not adequate to utter God, but it is the highest we have and we should use its highest words. The highest words in human speech are not high enough, but what do you gain by using lower words? or no words? It is for us to use the highest words we have, realize that they are not high enough, try to strain upwards from them, not to dredge human speech for something lower."[6] And one can gain nothing by ceasing to talk about God at all. It does not follow that because one has no idea what God's kingdom will be like ("eye hath not seen . . .") the phrase "Thy kingdom come" is meaningless; nor does it follow that because one has never seen God, that one cannot erect a system for talking about him.

Although language is inadequate to express the fullness of the godhead or our most profound and emotionful thoughts, it still contains more than enough meaning and potential for the vast majority of its users. Complaints about language are only really justified after one has tested its full potential, and few people concentrate so intensely as to get to the bottom of the words they use. How many, for example, have understood the profoundest thoughts it has been the privilege of language to express: the great works of the greatest authors? It is enough for human purposes that language can describe God "virtually". If due care is given to syntax and definition, constructive talk about God can be carried on; if one knows the limitations, one can avoid their distorting results. For example, the sentence "God made the world" can be criticized as inadequate and a distortion of reality, because the tense-form of the verb implies an activity which has been completed, whereas in fact God is still creating the world, or holding it in existence, which is better expressed as "God is making the world". This is true, but the insufficiency of "God made the world" does not mean that one cannot express the two facts together. It might be a

[6] F. Sheed, *Theology and Sanity*, p. 31.

more periphrastic statement than if there was a single verb form, such as "God made and is making the world", but it is nonetheless accurate. A similar argument exists for definition. A divine activity such as loving has no simple gloss, but this does not make such a concept meaningless: it may take a book to explain what is meant by God's love, but considerations of length of explanation are irrelevant in semantics.

There are two further points, arising from God's being ultimately the creator of language. Firstly, it would be a travesty of divine justice if man was expected to use language for purposes for which it was not capable. God knows when expression becomes strained, and would not condemn willingness: he does not expect miracles, only attention. Secondly, if language is his creation, he knows its limitations. But this has not stopped him using language to tell mankind the truth about himself: the Word used the word. Language, in the face of such evidence, could not have been an insuperable obstacle to truth, as the above objections suggested; rather, it must be the way to truth.

Discussion about whether it is possible to use language to talk about metaphysical truths well is largely a waste of time for three reasons. Firstly, no matter how much linguistic perfectibility was attained, there could still be only an inadequate knowledge of God for a human being. Secondly, what possible verifiable criterion could one set up for deciding when language has expressed a metaphysical truth *best* of all? A consensus of human opinion would be of little use, as judgements would be prejudiced by familiar norms of language. A valid criterion would have to be extra-linguistic—language cannot be used as the measure of its own success—and how does one go about setting up a supernatural criterion without language? Thirdly, and most important, an overconcentration on language form in religious matters involving fundamental truths is bad, because no amount of stylistic knowledge will eradicate a confused mind. If one knows clearly *what* one wants to say, one will find a way to say it. It is God who is too complex, not language which is too simple.

To avoid the danger of theological debate degenerating into questions of stylistics, and to reassert the ultimate aim of all linguistic analysis, more attention must be paid to understanding better the complexities of the language we already have and do use—even though it is inadequate and we use it badly. As implied above, language can lead to more meaning than the majority can understand. One must therefore make best use of the resources available, examining the potentialities of the medium, and removing as much "noise" as possible from the communication channel between the individual and God either by minimizing distractions or increasing one's knowledge of the linguistic medium through which the information is being presented. Some kind of systematic expression analysis is required to understand the abnormal usages which formalize more vividly the profundity of a spiritual meaning—grammatical discord, for example,[7] or paradox.[8] Above all, as we shall see, a sharpened consciousness is required to appreciate the relevance and power of imagery, which is contrived, purposeful special effect.

Anyone who wishes to use words in a didactic, analytic, persuasive or intense way needs to be aware of the potential power in language. Words are "dramatic ammunition" to Samuel Beckett, "hard as cannonballs" to Emerson, and "loaded pistols", which have to be fired very carefully, to Jean-Paul Sartre. Unclear theological writing is probably the most dangerous of all, and obscure preaching loses souls. The sound of words can distract the mind from their sense: the rhythm of a litany can hypnotize an attention away from its purpose, one can be mesmerized by the metrical beat of the *Confiteor* at a Dialogue Mass. It is the reversal of priorities to go to church to listen to the singing. To study the language of religion gives an increased understanding of what the religion is trying to do, of what lies behind its terminology, where potential obscurity lies, and what needs bringing up to date, for both external and internal consumption. It shows that quality is the relevant factor in prayer, not quantity. Finally, it shows that to be careless about language use, whether in praying or discussing, leads to confused thinking and distorted presentation: there is a modern tendency to play and ploy with words which is detrimental to religion, though it is all too frequently found there.

[7] Cf. above, p. 127.
[8] Cf. below, p. 177.

ON INTERPRETATION

The teaching of the Church is based on an oral tradition and a written text, which is the Bible; as a result, biblical studies are another field wherein close contact with linguistics would seem profitable. Such studies have received a powerful stimulus from the papal encyclicals of this century, which have emphasized the need for more research into the many spheres of Testament life to ascertain as conclusively as possible the psychological and environmental pressures acting upon the writers of Scripture. The relevance of linguistics should be clear upon reference to some of the important points made in these encyclicals, beginning with *Providentissimus Deus*. Here, Leo XIII clarified the basis of study. The first business of textual criticism is to decide upon a text. The Latin Vulgate is declared to be the "authentic" version, the meaning of the Hebrew and Greek being "substantially rendered" there; but where obscurity or ambiguity arises, the examination of older tongues would be advantageous. The study of Oriental languages and the art of textual criticism are to be the main lines of research. It is accepted that internal indications are often insufficient to settle a textual problem; historical problems require "the witness of history", internal evidence being confirmation.[9]

Pius XII, in *Divino Afflante Spiritu* (1943), summarized the lines modern research was to take. Many new finds had been made, of papyri, scrolls, codices, and so on. Knowledge of Greek and Hebrew had amassed considerably since the Renaissance; the scholar should know oriental languages, and should "support his interpretation by the aids which all branches of philology supply". The original text "has more authority and greater weight than any even the very best translation, whether ancient or modern".... Textual criticism primarily concerns itself with "the correction of the codices" (Augustine), to remove copyists' errors, glosses, omissions, misplaced words, and so on. Pius XII emphasized that the Tridentine Decree to use the Vulgate was only for public use in the Latin Church—it did

---

[9] Cf. St Jerome, Ep. 29, "When discussing Holy Scripture it is not words we want so much as the meaning of words", and the Preface to the 1611 Bible: "For is the Kingdom of God become words or syllables?"

not diminish the authority of the early texts. Finally, the semantic procedure to be adopted in textual criticism was affirmed: the literal meaning is to be discovered first, then the spiritual. "The supreme rule of interpretation is to discover and define what the writer intended to express", which requires understanding all the verbal and situational contextual pressures, and in particular, the mode of writing at the time.

Today there is the science of interpretation (hermeneutics), which aims to discover and expound the true meaning of scriptural language. Technically, it involves the three stages of *noematics* (the determination of the possible senses of Scripture), *heuristics* (the determination of the true meaning by a known set of rules), and *prophoristics* (the explanation of the text to others). The practical utilization of interpretative procedures is known as *exegesis*. Although there have been few texts which the Church has found it necessary to interpret offially, problems of interpretation are continually being placed in a new light, due to new discoveries of texts, additional contemporary language data, archaeological evidence, and so on. And many ancient problems still remain.

As such problems begin in language, and end with the verification of the meaning of that language, linguistics should be able to provide valuable assistance. As yet, however, little attempt has been made to apply the techniques of diachronic and synchronic linguistics to the pursuance of the aims of biblical interpretation. James Barr, in his recent book, talks about "the failure to relate what is said about either Hebrew or Greek to a general semantic method related to general linguistics" and the distortion which can result and has resulted from such ignorance.[10] The first task facing present-day linguists is to eradicate the mass of misconceptions, frequently referred to throughout the present book, which have affected any field where matters of language are important—and there are many cases (as Barr points out) where biblical scholars have followed certain invalid procedures. Only after this can the language-scholar begin to construct an adequate linguistic theory.

Firstly, the kinds of linguistic statement which have been made are usually of dubious significance because one does not

[10] *The Semantics of Biblical Language* (Oxford, 1961), p. 24.

know how to evaluate them: the lack of a complete and systematic description of any of the biblical languages using realistic linguistic procedures means that there is no way of incorporating isolated bits of language information proferred by various scholars into a general theory for the languages, which is prerequisite for any linguistic generalization at all. Different frameworks are used, different categories set up, different pieces of text used as evidence; often, the data used as the basis for the linguistic statement is not referred to (though the way the results are phrased sometimes implies that the *whole* of the language has been examined) and as a result it becomes difficult to compare the work of different authors, or even of the same author in different articles.

All too often, the attention and interest of an author is attracted to certain features of the language which have been traditionally assumed to be important or "characteristic", or which have something unique about them, and the remainder of the language is ignored. There are two points at issue here. Firstly, such a procedure can only give a distorted impression of the language, as it concentrates on the features which seem odd or important to the (necessarily) biased mind of the researcher, who is usually trying to prove a point of religious significance. Before one can make statements about characteristic language patterns in the data, everything must be systematically described, and the norms for the language set up, through a formal description which is carried out regardless of the status of the evidence, the aims of the researcher, and what we know about the non-linguistic climate of the times. Only in this way can the danger of preconceptions be avoided, and the problems of a distorted description be overcome.

If one knows what one is looking for, it is usually not difficult to find evidence for it somewhere in the data of a language. Which brings us to the second point, that when one does begin with preconceptions about the Hebrew "mind" or "way of thinking", one naturally tends to emphasize the corroborative evidence and to ignore other contradictory features:

> It is this starting from the theoretical end, from the assurance of understanding the Hebrew mind, and working from there to its linguistic form, that causes the haphazardness of modern theological treatments of linguistic evidence. A person deeply

conscious of the features of the Hebrew mind will notice some linguistic feature which illustrates it. He does not search about to see if there are other features which point in the opposite direction; and if there are still others which do not openly bear the stamp of the Hebrew mind, they are presumably "neutral" facts which have nothing to say one way or the other. Thus, since a systematic examination or description of the language is not being done, a few phenomena which illustrate the theory seem to be striking confirmation of it, and what were occasional and possible illustrative examples come to appear as a total system corresponding to the realities of Hebrew thought. The theory thus becomes presumptive evidence for the interpretation of facts that are doubtful.[11]

The same argument can apply for the other biblical languages; it is a common fallacious procedure outside of biblical studies also. This is really another instance of meaning-based analysis, starting with sense and proceeding from there to sound, a procedure which is valid only when the situation from which one is starting is relatively clear-cut and definable (cf. onomasiology above). When one is dealing in concepts such as "a Hebrew consciousness of time" (as opposed to a Greek), the "uniqueness" of Hebrew thought, the "correctness" of certain ideas, and so on, "proving" these from the language data, then the procedure is particularly suspect.

> It is possible to see great difficulties in the idea . . . that the "unique character" of a people finds its expression in its language. One has here to avoid the vague and unscientific generalizations often made about nations and their languages. When people observe the behaviour and character of a nation they also observe their ways of speech, and naturally they associate these closely with one another. It is another thing to suppose that for features of character observed it will be possible to see corresponding patterns in the linguistic structure when analysed in itself. And even if it may be possible to see such relations occasionally in particular, this does not entitle us to begin by taking as an obviously valid instrument of investigation the idea that a language is a full expression of the national character.[12]

As discussed in Chapter VII, one must not be too Whorfian in assuming the uniqueness or otherwise of a language's

[11] Barr, *op. cit.*, p. 23.   [12] Barr, *op. cit.*, pp. 40–1.

thought. One often hears statements of the form "Language X has a word for it, but Y has not" therefore "X can say something Y cannot", or "X is a better language than Y". This fallacy stems from the misconception, already discussed, that the unit of translation equivalence between languages is the word; in actual fact it is the sentence, which is the main meaning-carrier in context. The fact that Y has no word for an object does not mean that it cannot talk about that object; it cannot use the same mechanical means to do so, but it can utilize alternative forms of expression in its own structure for the same end. It is the aim of a translator to make sentence equal sentence, to give sense for sense, and only a small part of the sense would appear in a word-for-word translation, especially if the languages were not closely related. If one compared the vocabulary of two languages in this way, then the conclusion that each language embodies a unique thinking-system is inescapable; but it is not legitimate to isolate words in this way.

Finally, the argument that there is some kind of natural parallel between grammar and thought is extremely unlikely, in view of similarities of temperament occurring alongside great dissimilarities in structure, and *vice versa*. Also, the high frequency of loanwords and the fact of large numbers of successful translations would also go against any rigid theory of uniqueness of thought in language. Naturally, assumptions about uniqueness are the cause of much interpretative confusion, as different sources are ascribed to the uniqueness; it is not difficult to find corroborative evidence for contradictory theories in a text. The only way to resolve such contradictions is to compare the disparate information in the light of a general linguistic theory, within which statistical and other techniques have established structural norms for the language as a whole. The first business of the biblical linguist is description.

The second major issue concerns the favoured technique of making comparative linguistic statements without adequate preparation. There are a number of potential errors here. An author might, for example, analyse Greek using one linguistic theory, analyse Hebrew using another, then compare the two without taking the theoretical differences (which would involve definition of descriptive terminology) into consideration; one thus finds parallels which are not really there, and fails to find

correlations which do exist. Also, unless one uses the same linguistic theory for all analysis, there is little possibility of correlating any results: it is difficult enough providing one consistent
and adequate theory, let alone providing two and having to
devise means whereby they can be evaluated against each other.
Thus, while there are a number of well-tried techniques of
description available, only one should be chosen, and this then
kept as a yardstick against which the formal features of both
languages can be measured. In this way, the differences between
them become clearly and realistically apparent. What is particularly invalid is to use one language as a norm, against which
one plots the patterns of the other language, and displays
"exceptions" there. This is ultimately a distorting view of both
languages, which can only be corrected by reference to a theory
which is more general than either language. To compare Greek
to Latin without a more embracing theory is to accentuate the
differences and ignore the similarities. A distant perspective
must always be available to correct the errors arising from too
close a view.

Untested semantic hypotheses used to explain the meaning of
biblical passages can therefore be very dangerous, especially
when made the basis of theological conclusions. Before one can
utilize linguistic evidence from Scripture, it must be carefully
weighed in its own linguistic terms. There must be a systematic,
synchronic description of the grammatical and lexical patterns of
a language before the more important contextualization can be
carried out. Norms must be established and stylistic effects
peculiar to a particular text determined before in later work
one begins to make cross-cultural comparisons, and to define
theological and sociological patterns in terms of linguistic
criteria. At all stages, an awareness of linguistic principles is
very necessary, otherwise one begins to make decisions based
on invalid inference. An example of this is the over-reliance on
etymological information in the determination of synchronic
meanings. The derivation of a word is irrelevant for determining the current meaning of a word at any given time, though it
is a commonly heard traditional argument that the earliest
meaning a word has should be a guide to the way the word
should be used. Appeals to etymology are dramatic, but irrelevant; the "basic" or "correct" meaning of a word depends on a

statistical survey of its uses,[13] not in what it used to mean or what one individual thinks it ought to mean. Such normativism, unfortunately, can be found in certain biblical exegetical texts.[14]

There are further specific problems in textual analysis of scriptural data. The difficulties of description are accentuated by the long period of authorship (possibly 1270 B.C.–A.D. 100), which would require not one but a series of descriptions, to take account of linguistic change. Again, the insufficiency of additional Aramaic and Hebrew texts to satisfactorily confirm decisions as to the linguistic character and meaning of the biblical texts is an important limitation, particularly when the question is one of typical senses, detection of copyist errors, and the like. There is little contemporary material available, and that which exists often embodies contradictory readings. Detailed philological work is necessary (and is being done) to resolve linguistic confusion with such a paucity of texts; palaeographic and cryptographic techniques are often essential.

The corpus of data is gradually increasing, however, bringing new languages as well as more information about familiar languages: Ancient Egyptian and Akkadian were only deciphered in the nineteenth century, Ugaritic was discovered in 1929, and more recently, there has been the Dead Sea Scrolls, and the work of Michael Ventris and others on Linear B. Unfortunately, the texts have a widely scattered distribution, in time as well as space, and hence are of various degrees of relevance for any biblical text. Also, much of the evidence necessary before a comparative description could be carried out has not yet been published, though the amount is increasing in rough proportion to financial support, and material is usually readily available for interested scholars. Thirdly, once a linguistic description has been carried out, the Eastern authorship and milieu present difficulties to scholars who are largely Western. An ignorance of specialized literary forms can lead to profound misunderstandings of scriptural passages—the confusion over the biblical account of Genesis in relation to evolution, for example. It is normally not possible to deduce the meaning of a literary

---

[13] The same technique is used in dictionary-making.
[14] Cf. Barr, *op. cit.*, Chapter VI, for a selection of excellent examples of this.

form from internal evidence, and supporting historical, archaeological or linguistic evidence becomes necessary.

The importance of a correct assessment of the literary forms
used in Scripture must not be underestimated. A literary form
is an accepted way of writing or speaking at a given time in a
given culture; and the fact that a writer might be inspired does
not affect his literary habits. Pius XII, in his encyclical, stressed
that much of the misunderstanding of the Bible was due to a
failure to appreciate the older literary techniques: "Quite often
when the sacred writers have been accused of an historical error
or an inaccuracy in what they have recorded, a closer examination has shown that they were only expressing themselves in a
conventional form of narration that was normal in the everyday
life of those ancient times and sanctioned by common usage."
Each text must be considered in the light of its special purpose
within its own temporal and geographical context, if the nature
of the permanent religious truths is to be at all apprehended.
There should be no reading in a perspective of modern scientific knowledge to the work of the sacred writers, and then
criticizing them for incompatibility or inaccuracy, for example,
in talking about a solid firmament or a flat earth. And the
different styles must not be judged by irrelevant linguistic
criteria. The imaginative language of poetry, for example, must
not be interpreted as if it were literal; the language of non-
scientific, popular description must not be judged by scientific
criteria—this would be like condemning a "sunrise" as being
strictly untrue. Figures of speech are normal in certain contexts,
and must be recognized as such. Our Lord's parables are not
meant to be judged using the same criteria as the historical
narrative of, say, the Acts of the Apostles or the Gospels, which
use a linguistic style suitable for recorded history. One must
also learn to recognize the highly imaginative descriptions
typical of apocalypse, for example, and the deliberate exaggera-
tions of historical fact that would be an important characteristic
of midrash. Paradoxes must not be dismissed as meaningless,[15]
and different types of symbols must be differentiated.

Finally, the criterion of a spiritual (or typical) meaning is
quite distinct from the literal meaning of a text. The latter is

[15] Cf. below, p. 177.

the norm, comprehending the immediate meanings of ordinary language, metaphor, parable, and so on; its elucidation is the primary semantic task. The former determines types, that is, prefigurations of a later person or event, such as Adam and Christ, Eve and Mary, the flood and Baptism. They are different from ordinary symbols, in that the type has a meaning in reality apart from its function as a type. It has a different kind of literary existence from the literal meaning, and different again from the *sensus plenior*, the meaning added to a retrospectively-interpreted statement, such as a prophecy about Christ, which the sacred writer could not have consciously intended. All these variations in type have corresponding variations in form, which characterize them, and it is only by finding formal criteria that one can avoid the intrusion of too many "accommodated senses"—or meanings read in by the modern reader. Everything can appear to be a symbol if one thinks for long enough; but there are symbolic names, visions, numbers and actions enough in Scripture without increasing their number.

Finally, a thorough linguistic description can clear up a number of problems of detail: it will point to usage to remove commonly held misinterpretations, such as making "first-born son" imply that Mary had more children, or "brethren" mean that Jesus had brothers, or "woman" indicate that Jesus was showing coldness towards his mother—all the result of reading meanings into older forms which did not contain such implications. It can assist in the production of better translations, the detection of errors, and the removal of one's own ignorance of the practices of the times, the results of which could only produce increasing support for the words of Augustine to St Jerome (Ep. 82): "And if in these books I meet anything which seems contrary to truth, I shall not hesitate to conclude either that the text is faulty, or that the translator has not expressed the meaning of the passage, or that I myself do not understand."

CHAPTER XI

LANGUAGE AND THE LITURGY

What is the connection between prayer and language? Is it necessary to have words to pray? Such questions are fairly common. The Catechism definition of prayer makes no explicit mention of language: prayer is defined as the raising up of the mind and heart to God; it is the sole form of communication (some say communion) with him. But the question must immediately arise, How does one begin to raise up the mind in this way? And this is where language enters in.

There is private, personal prayer, and there is public, shared prayer; a distinction is necessary. Now mechanical help is needed for all kinds of private prayer except possibly the momentary, impulsive offering, and the intense, yet at the same time simple contemplation of the mystic; this naturally takes the form of words, which are the most useful and expressive tools of communication. It has been argued that all "higher" forms of thought require some verbalization at a sub-vocal level, and prayer, in the sense of a deliberately framed communicative activity, would be included in this. This is also the most frequently occurring kind of prayer; literally "thought-less" prayers (such as contemplation) are best seen as the exception. Intense mental activity without the aid of words does not come naturally to many, and as the Church has never been limited to an intellectual or mystically-gifted few, it recommends that more attention is paid to language in trying to communicate with God: hence suggestions for prayer "with the lips", "ejaculations", and other means of getting into the habit of "talking" to God, are seen as important ways of alleviating a very real problem. The difficulties, of course, depend upon and vary among individuals and the degree to which they follow a spiritual life, and require no general legislation on the part of the Church—only advice as to how the greatest benefit might be obtained through the use of private language. Much more complex is the relationship between public prayer, the liturgy, and the public language which plays such an important part in it, because although this too has to be functional and devotional (as with private prayer), it must also be acceptable by all who wish to use it, and in line with the teaching of the Church. It thus requires legislation; and every linguist knows the difficulties inherent in laying down the law about language.

From one point of view, the liturgy is a set of procedures given formal realization by the Church for promoting reciprocal communication between the individual and God. It involves both conventional and symbolic activity, and requires a threefold participation, of God, the individual and the Church. Using a communication analogy, the triadic nature of the operation is clear, for the liturgy is a channel which transmits the aspirations of an individual via the Church's blessing to God, and, if conditions are fulfilled, allows the return of sanctifying grace. If any one of the participants failed in its function, then the liturgical act would be ineffective. As always, the proper channels must be followed if communication is to be successful; and in the liturgy the sensible result of the communicative activity is signs: "the sanctification of man is signified by signs perceptible to the senses, and is effected in a way which corresponds with each of these signs".[1]

Liturgical signs are usually of a visual or oral/aural character; senses of smell and touch, such as with incense and anointing, are less frequently involved. Words and visual activity reinforce and supplement each other, and point to the presence of a deeper, underlying spiritual activity. Of all the signs, however, language has the most central rôle to play; it is exceptional to discover acts of public worship without it. One of the purposes of the recent Vatican Council's recommendations is "that the intimate connection between words and rites may be

---

[1] Constitution on the Sacred Liturgy, trans. C. Howell, S.J., 7.

apparent in the liturgy"; [2] another is that active participation on the part of the people might be promoted by encouraging them "to take part by means of acclamations, responses, psalmody, antiphons and hymns, as well as by actions, gestures and bodily attitudes".[3]

If language has such a leading part in liturgical activity, then, as well as in other branches of the Church's work, it is of the highest importance that the type of language used should be carefully chosen and subjected to a thorough examination—in view of the "sound and smoke" endemic in much of language.[4] Any suggestion that a liturgical language should be modified must be reviewed bearing in mind the total relevant liturgical, doctrinal and cultural implications, for radical ideas to do with sacred traditions are always going to be unpopular. Acceptance of a change, because of its universal application, must be preceded by careful study, and receive a general, hierarchic consent; sporadic implementation fosters disunity and confusion. The Vatican Council has recently accepted in principle the need for such a change in liturgical expression. The decision came after a long period of controversy, which still continues, if muted.

THE PRINCIPLES OF A LITURGICAL LANGUAGE

A liturgical language is a particular set of forms, either a style or a whole language, used in official public worship on behalf of a religion. It was normal for a culture to have two languages; one, the language of everyday, the other, the sacred language, reserved for use by a few people on a sacred occasion. And today, it is still necessary for a religion to have a special, "marked" style to highlight its specialized purpose. This is a formally abnormal kind of language which one does not normally use or expect, and in its unfamiliarity lies its value, for it attracts attention to the exceptional purpose of its function. An unfamiliar style is used for any social situation which requires more than an everyday "language of little

[2] *Constitution*, 35.
[3] *Constitution*, 30.
[4] Cf. above, p. 120. For language in theology, see Chapter XII; language and biblical studies, Chapter X. Most examples will be taken from English in this and the following chapters, as this will be the language most familiar to the majority of readers.

effort". In talking to superiors, addressing a meeting, reading the news, writing an essay or an important letter, we realize, whether we like it or not, that ordinary, colloquial language will not do; it will not suit the purpose or the situation, and so we look round in our minds or in dictionaries for "better", more appropriate words. In general, the care we take over our language is in direct proportion to the importance we give to the situation, which usually means the person whom we are addressing. To be inconsistent, or to take no care at all, is incongruous. From the liturgical point of view, to the believer, there is obviously no limit to the care one should take while communicating, for the status of the recipient is supreme.[5] The needs of this situation are quite incompatible with the colloquial speech with which one addresses friends and acquaintances in relatively unimportant domestic situations. A familiar tone of voice is out of place in a divine context. "Whom seek ye?" is more in keeping than "Who're you looking for?"

While it is futile to make the language of the liturgy the same as everyday speech, it is even more futile to go to the other extreme, by adopting a style of language so esoteric that its users cannot understand it. An extremely archaic diction, or a completely foreign tongue, used without due cause, would lead to the linguistic mortal sin of unintelligibility, for it is an injustice to expect a society to worship in a language which it does not understand. Comprehensibility is the primary criterion. In older times, sacred languages were often partially or totally obscure (for example, the Vedic hymns), as was much of the poetry used in ancient ceremonies. This unintelligibility was not functionless in those days, however; rather, it added a mystical attraction to the activity by its obscurity. The high-sounding phrases were obviously great magic to the word-conscious tribes.[6] Today, people are no longer prepared to follow a deliberately obscure language; nor, in the case of Catholicism, are they expected to do so: "the

[5] There is also the point that the believer is usually eager to be careful.

[6] One of the functions of language, of course, is its use for the purpose of concealing thoughts, cf. above, p. 113. It occurs in the slang of cliques when faced by outsiders, Cockney rhyming slang, thieves' argot, cryptographies, children's language and doctor's prescriptions—all uses with their own logic.

rites ... should be within the people's powers of comprehension, and normally should not require much explanation."[7]

The liturgical language is a major part of a religion's "house-style".[8] Ideally, it needs to be sufficiently removed from ordinary language to be characterized and respected as God's, but without reducing intelligibility too greatly. It has to be unique, and not confusable with any other style, because this would only lead to profanity and carelessness in worship. It is therefore something the lay public must take time and trouble over, to learn how to get the most out of its use. There are various pamphlets, commentaries, textbooks and newspapers which can aid in this exegetical work. It is not enough to rely on the weekly sermon as an answer to everything. Spiritual reading is essential. The learning of the actual language is relatively easy; each of us has already learned a great number of completely unique kinds of language, to suit a corresponding number of social situations, which are rarely confused. It is learning to appreciate why the language is used that is the more difficult task. A new language cannot fill the gap created by doctrinal ignorance.

An introductory examination of what is involved in English religious language has been carried out elsewhere.[9] It has shown that there are four main characterizing elements to be distinguished, which need to be considered separately in assessing any liturgical position. These are formal stylistic features (for example, complex sentences, more "careful" enunciation and conservative syntactic forms) that place religious language at the correct end of the stylistic spectrum along with other kinds of "official" language; secondly, characteristic features of register, comprising archaisms (both in grammar and lexis), formu-

---

[7] *Constitution*, 34. Obscurity, of course, is by no means the same thing as the emotive power of words; the suggestivity of liturgical language is an important part of its effect. To cut out the emotional element in translation is to bow too far in the direction of objective clarity; the Bible begins to read like a newspaper report. Cf. Robert Graves' criticisms of the New English Bible in *Observer* for March 19th, 1961.

[8] And can therefore be changed when circumstances require it.

[9] D. Crystal, "A liturgical language in a linguistic perspective", *New Blackfriars*, December 1964.

laic utterance (which may subsume archaisms) that has arisen due to the traditional way of phrasing certain concepts, and specialized non-archaic vocabulary, used only in a religious context, which can also be classified into different kinds. Needless to say, any criticism of one aspect of religious language need not necessarily apply to other features within the same register because the criteria of use are different in each case. From this initial approach, it is clear that English has considerable resources for a more formal, heightened style such as is needed for liturgical language, and that most of this is quite acceptable to the majority as its roots lie deep within the English language.

Concerning the choice of a liturgical language, then, the following suggestions (*not* prescriptions) might help to resolve some of the dilemmas which arise over stylistic considerations —not, be it noted, for problems over sense.

1. Colloquial contractions of the day, slang, loosely-phrased language, vogue-words, and so on, typical of informal speech, should be avoided. Similarly, in areas of grammar where usage is changing, it is wise to retain the more formal pattern: "whom" for "who" as object in relative position, and so on.

2. While it is necessary for the language to run as smoothly as possible, to fulfil its function without undue distraction from the elements of form, the following formal factors should be considered:

   a. In scriptural texts and commonly-known prayers, formulaic utterance or traditionally loved and quoted phrases should be kept, as one is fighting a losing battle and causing unnecessary confusion trying to replace them. In texts being translated for general use for the first time, there will normally be little point in introducing an archaism;

   b. When the content would be unaffected by using either of a choice of synonyms, then the one to be chosen is that which is least used in other styles of the language, and which, being the more unfamiliar, has the most remote overtones.

3. All decisions, of course, must be made bearing in mind the

various contextual considerations which are relevant.[10] One translation in one context might well seem out-of-place in another, for a variety of reasons. "Thou", for example, must not be forced into every place, regardless of its function.

4. Some attempt must be made to find out what kinds of change would encounter most resistance, and where such resistance would arise; otherwise recommendations will be unrealistic. Points under 2a would be of particular importance here. Also, one should remember that while the most frequently occurring liturgical services (which involve a high proportion of formulaicness) will be the most resistant to change, changes once made will also be the most quickly assimilated. To lessen the shock of novelty, then, a gradual introduction of innovations is essential in every case.[11]

5. The most difficult, and perhaps the least important consideration is that of aesthetics, which requires that the results are as beautiful as they can be. This is most difficult, because of the impossibility of pleasing everyone's sense of aesthetic values; and least important, because the beauty of a liturgy is ancillary to its utilitarian purposes, and the language must be primarily geared to this. Charges of ugliness infrequently crop up in the forms of religious language, however, because their long histories have usually brought a large measure of acceptance. The "thou"-type cases are a small minority.

The introduction of a satisfactory vernacular, then, is a long and detailed business. The above suggestions require a large amount of minute linguistic description and analysis for satisfactory results: one needs a knowledge of the forms of language and the pragmatics of language.[12] This, then, is where the professional linguist can and should help the Church: he can provide information about how languages work, what resources they have, how they can be described, how people are likely to react, and how languages influence them—this would be an essential perspective for a realistic and permanent liturgical vernacular. Otherwise, decisions will be made in the dark.

[10] Cf. above, pp. 99–101. In particular, in translation, one must remember that it is the sentence which is the unit to be equated, not the word; a word-for-word translation is very inadequate.
[11] The *Constitution* provides scope for fulfilment of points 3 and 4.
[12] Also an awareness of the fact of linguistic change.

There is plenty of time for such background research. The impatience of many at the slow speed of introduction of various changes is unwise: a language cannot be shifted from a sociocultural situation overnight after 1500 years of use. One needs a transition period, often of years, for new linguistic habits to develop; and new words need time before they cease being a distraction to ancient rites, and become an acceptable part of them.

Finally, there should be no question of a fundamental opposition between Latin and the vernacular. How much vernacular to introduce, and where to introduce it are decisions which, as we have seen, must be made in their own liturgical context, keeping doctrinal implications closely in mind: arguments must always be resolved in dogma, not in aesthetics or history alone. To ignore context is to put language in a vacuum again. Practical considerations are also important—what need to translate the silent parts of the Mass, for example?[13] Decisions must be based on the needs of the diocese, and there are many possible schemes available, such as utilizing pilot surveys to test reaction, having half the Sunday Masses use some of the innovations, and so on. Translation, it must be concluded, is not the panacea it has been made out to be. While words need to be understood, so must the activities which they accompany, and both must achieve some degree of fusion. Unthinking loyalties to either Latin or the vernacular are useless and indefensible. There is already the Kyrie in Greek, after all, and the Trisagion on Good Friday; the Alleluia and Amen in Hebrew; and in the papal High Mass, both Epistle and Gospel are read in Greek as well as Latin. The liturgy is already partly cosmopolitan; the vernacular is only a difference of degree.

---

[13] One could argue this on the grounds of the priest's greater facility in his native language, and that a greater impression of functional unity might be given if the language of the whole Mass was as near uniform as possible. On the other hand, a linguistic change might emphasize more satisfactorily the climax which is approaching. A full treatment of both viewpoints would, however, require us to enter into a discussion of the whole range of arguments pro- and anti-Latin, pro- and anti-vernacular (four views which must be distinguished for clear and constructive debate)—clearly a subject too large for this book. Cf. Bibliography under Cunliffe and Küng.

CHAPTER XII

LANGUAGE AND LOGICAL POSITIVISM

THE POSITIVIST ATTACK

It seems impossible these days (perhaps it always has been) to carry on any kind of conceptual discussion without someone raising a question of definition. The "higher" the level of the argument, the more likely this becomes. Philosophical problems nearly always resolve at some stage into a discussion of the meaning of terms. "It all depends what you mean by . . ." has long been a typical and useful gambit; it reached its logical conclusion in "it all depends what you mean by meaning".[1] Matters of definition, however, at least overlap with the linguist's province. The basis of definition is clearly a matter of the way certain terms are used; and such knowledge is only really derivable from a synchronic linguistic description of a large number of *paroles*. Intuition is an unreliable norm. As was discussed earlier,[2] grammars and dictionaries, which purport to describe the way words are used and which are really recommendations or rules for further usage, are only valid in so far as they are themselves based on and up-to-date with usage. A dictionary modelled on the ideas of a Humpty Dumpty would be pointless because unusable.[3] All linguistic disputes and judgements about "what people say" must ultimately be resolved by reference to definable facts of usage; and argument

---

[1] Cf. *The Meaning of Meaning.*
[2] See above, p. 81.
[3] Lewis Carroll, "When I use a word, it means just what I choose it to mean—neither more nor less".

of any kind based on definitions must first determine whether the definition proposed is generally acceptable or a deliberate departure (nonce usage) from the norm of common educated parlance. Otherwise there will never be any constructive thinking.

Over the past few decades, many philosophers have come to realize that their concern with words was not marginal, in the nature of a final resort in discussion, but of central interest. Language has become the focal point of attention as never before. The relevance of such a movement from the point of view of this book becomes immediately obvious when one finds such a statement as "all utterances about the nature of God are nonsensical" coming as the result of arguing along lines suggested by one branch of the new orientation. This was one effect of Logical Positivism. It is no longer a popular position to maintain, but some of its ideas live on in modified form, and much of the confusion caused by its presence is still evident. The strange thing is, that although the theory stands or falls by its assumptions about language, there has been little thorough criticism of its principles and procedures from a linguistic point of view—a surprising omission, as forceful generalizations about language occupy so much of its canon. This chapter is but one approach to the subject, from the linguistic rather than the philosophical point of view, which attempts to highlight some of the more glaring fallacies, and draw together some of the strands of critical opinion that have been suggested from time to time as displaying the misleading nature of logical positivism. For although claiming the support of usage, many of the issues resolve into an egocentric linguistic abusage.

It is difficult to discuss logical positivism these days with complete consistency. Since its official inception in 1929, there have been many variant forms, and the teaching of its original exponents has sometimes been much modified—at times, in the face of certain telling criticisms, retracted. As C. E. M. Joad said: "Whatever statement of logical positivism one takes, one runs the risk of being told that it is out of date or that it represents a deviationist view".[4] And in view of the many popular titles that have been attributed to what is fundamentally the

---

[4] *A Critique of Logical Positivism* (London, 1950), p. 16.

same theory—Logical Analysis, Philosophical Analysis, Metaphysical Analysis even—this is not surprising. A detailed
survey, also, would have to distinguish it from the later and
much less headstrong Linguistic Analysis, which differed from
it in a number of important respects. From the point of view of
this chapter, it is perhaps permissible to generalize a little,
making "logical positivism", for the sake of brevity and simplicity refer to a mentality that underlay many philosophers'
statements, while not being explicitly correlated in its totality
with any one of them. While many, for example, would emphasize
the status of language and the verificational principle (for which
see below), not everyone would accept that all metaphysical
utterances are meaningless.[5] Certainly these days most British
philosophers could not justly be labelled "logical positivist".

What to choose, then, as the basis for discussion here? It is
generally accepted that the most popular and influential book
expounding the main tenets of the positivist system in English,
while differing in certain respects from the continental model,
was *Language, Truth and Logic* by A. J. Ayer, published in
1936, and revised, with some important modifications, in 1946.
One article once gave it "almost the status of a philosophic
Bible"—an analogy which would probably have been dismissed
as meaningless by Ayer himself, but which still gives some idea
of its force. It was certainly the most dramatic in its expression
of the new view, and most dogmatic in its insistence on the
necessity for intellectual modernization. Its currency was aided
by its being in English, and it has been the basis of much of the
discussion in English-speaking circles. The two editions of this
book will therefore form the main examples for this chapter. In
view of the selectivity of the survey, which does not do the book
justice, or its critics, and the linguistic, rather than philosophical
or theological orientation, the reader is referred to the referential footnote, which is indispensable for further elucidation.

The movement itself began at Vienna in 1922, when Moritz
Schlick became Professor. The "Vienna Circle" formed itself,
as a loose kind of organization to talk about matters of common
interest, composed of a number of leading European philo-

[5] Cf. Ayer's later position, referred to on p. 184; and Russell, in
History of Western Philosophy: "complete metaphysical agnosticism is
not compatible with the maintenance of linguistic propositions".

sophers, mathematicians, logicians and scientists. A great deal of activity followed. Their first international congress was held in 1929; this was followed by the publication of their journal *Erkenntis* (later, *The Journal of United Sciences*) in 1930. Ayer joined in 1933. Three years later, Schlick was murdered by a student; shortly afterwards, the Second World War began; and the Circle broke up. It has never been re-established, and its ideas live on only in the views of isolated philosophers in all parts of the world. Naturally, opinions are considerably diverse these days.

Philosophers had, of course, been specifically interested in language before, linguistic problems being as endemic as they are. A kind of linguistic analysis appears in Plato, Aristotle and Aquinas, for example, even though the philosophers who practised it may not always have known that they were doing so.[6] And in a loose sense, any kind of discussion which begins with elucidation of terms, and the like, could be called a linguistic analysis. It is the explicit reliance on language which differentiates logical positivism from earlier interest, as well as the logical rigour with which it was constructed from ideas of such men as Comte, Mill, Mach, Leibniz, Frege, Russell, Whitehead, Einstein and Wittgenstein—a few of the figures the Circle named in 1929 as intellectual forebears. It was clear that much influence derived from those philosophers commonly known as representative of the British tradition of empiricist philosophy: Locke, Berkeley, Hume and Mill. All had the principle in common that the sole valid criterion of knowledge was personal sense experience, and all as a result rejected *a prioristic* first principles, and metaphysics as a whole. Auguste Comte's (1797–1857) brand of positivism was similar: the physical and social sciences provided all verifiable knowledge, and intellectual activity was legitimate only if directed towards the methodical classification of sense data. The object of philosophy, then, was in the world, where it had usually been: the philosopher looked at referents, and tried to make them cohere.

The modern formulation of positivist principles was an attempt to meet the growing dissatisfaction with the state of philosophical studies, in particular to answer the question,

---

[6] See Copleston, *Contemporary Philosophy* (London, 1956), pp. 1–3.

What was philosophy for? The advent of more scientific disciplines during the post-Industrial Revolution period, and the widening of their scope, meant that there was little, if any empirical data left for the philosopher to study. What, then, could the philosopher do? If he could not investigate the world, as he was wont, it seemed he was redundant. It was affirmed by many that "philosophy is not one of the natural sciences".[7] With Kantian influence still strong, metaphysics was an unpopular alternative. Ethics smacked too much of psychology. And the concept of a rôle for philosophy as super-synthesizer of all subjects, as was occasionally suggested, was out of the question on the obvious grounds that, even supposing such a synthesis were possible, no one would possess the required brain capacity.

The Vienna Circle argued that there was one thing all sciences had in common that could be delimited: language. All sciences used language as a means of expression and communication.[8] Some used it well; others badly. Many used it badly without realizing it, and hence produced further confusion for themselves. It became clear that here was where philosophy's true function lay, in a study of the usage of language forms, and of their meanings. Philosophy was to be talk about talk: "The propositions of philosophy are not factual, but linguistic in character—that is, they do not describe the behaviour of physical, or even mental, objects; they express definitions, or the formal consequences of definitions".[9] A little later (p. 59), the switch in interest from referent to language is emphasized: "We may speak loosely of him (the philosopher) as analyzing facts, or notions, or even things. But we must make it clear that these are simply ways of saying that he is concerned with the definition of the corresponding words."

The influence of the earlier philosophers is very clear. Locke, for example, had this to say: "Perhaps if ideas and words were distinctly weighed and duly considered, they would afford us another sort of logic and critique than what we have hitherto been acquainted with".[10] Then there were G. E. Moore and

[7] Wittgenstein, *Tractatus*, 4. 111.
[8] Cf. Condillac, "Une science n'est qu'une langue bien faite."
[9] *Language, Truth and Logic* (London, 1946), p. 57.
[10] *An Essay Concerning Human Understanding*, IV, 21, iv.

Bertrand Russell, whose ideas had a more immediate influence on the reification of terminology and analysis (as opposed to the idealistic synthesizing of F. H. Bradley). But much more immediately influential was Ludwig Wittgenstein, who presented the new view as he might a revelation:

Tractatus Philosophicus:
"4.002.   Language disguises thought ...
4.003.   Most of the propositions and questions to be found in philosophical works are not false but nonsensical.
4.0031. All philosophy is a 'critique of language'...
4.112.   A philosophical work consists essentially of elucidations ... the clarification of propositions."

The Vienna Circle built on such premises. There were two related issues. On the one hand, there was this profound dissatisfaction with traditional philosophy which, in all but a few instances, was condemned for obscurity, word-spinning or superstition. On the other hand, there was the dogmatic and radical emphasis on language as the essential object (and the only one) of philosophical study. So much for the accumulated wisdom of generations! Ayer covers Plato onwards in his first sentence: "The traditional disputes of philosophers are, for the most part, as unwarranted as they are unfruitful".[11] Instead, the scope of philosophy was to be narrowed but made more precise: "If the philosopher is to uphold his claim to make a special contribution to the stock of our knowledge, he must not attempt to formulate speculative truths, or to look for first principles, or to make *a priori* judgements about the validity of our empirical beliefs. He must, in fact, confine himself to works of clarification and analysis" (p. 51) ... "to elicit the consequences of our linguistic usages" (p. 133).[12]

So to the poet's question "What's in a name?" the positivist answered "Everything". The tool of philosophy was no longer to be mind but language. "All our philosophy is improvement about language" (Lichtenberg). "The philosophy of a science is

[11] *Op. cit.*, p. 33. Much of this early intolerance was to disappear in the course of time, but its original influence was great.
[12] The task of the philosopher is "the detection of the sources in linguistic idioms of current misconceptions and absurd things". (G. Ryle, "Systematically Misleading Expressions".)

the syntactic analysis of the language of that science" (R. Carnap). "Logical" was added to the title, because the school hoped to incorporate the findings of modern logic and mathematics into their system. The field lay open before them, with vast quantities of data awaiting a method of analysis. The problems language posed were clear—problems such as contradiction, tautology, obscurity and ambiguity, which led continually to apparent conflicts between theories and disciplines. By a close examination of the linguistic facts of "ordinary language", it was felt, many problems could be solved by showing them to be baseless, residing merely in verbiage. This would be the major application of the positivist method.

Although Wittgenstein's own approach was more empirically orientated, more a careful inspection of facts than a linguistic analysis, his inspiration lies behind much of the positivist nominalism. He, and Russell before him, claimed that there were a number of elementary statements in language which (if true) corresponded to simple facts. All other valid uses of language were then based on these. These basic statements were *propositions* (units of meaning or "pictures of reality")[13] and it was the business of the philosopher to analyse and discuss them. A proposition was the rôle played by a sentence, a sequence of grammatically related words. It had to be a sequence, being a definition, which (by definition) needs more than one word to exist. The importance of context was thus realized as crucial in any discussion of meaning: "Only the proposition has sense; only in the nexus of a proposition has a name meaning". (*Tractatus*, 3. 3.)[14]

Linguistic study of this kind was not a synthesis; as it began with complex units of meaning, it could only be an analysis. The purpose of the analysis then was to point out the difficulties

[13] *Tractatus*, 4. 01.
[14] It was a limitation of the theory that it did not extend the notion of context to stretches of language longer than the proposition and to styles as a whole. This was probably the reason for much of the later misorientated criticism of metaphysical language: the *total* linguistic background for such propositions as "God exists" was ignored; but many such propositions only derive their full meaning from an understanding of linguistic interrelationships larger than the sentence. Cf. Chapter VIII and below, pp. 173, ff.

underlying a consistent use of language forms, which would clarify understanding and expression (e.g. for research workers who are forced to communicate their specialist findings to a non-specialist public), and also suggest ways of producing more logical languages. Ayer outlines his procedure: "A complete philosophical elucidation of any language would consist, first, in enumerating the types of sentence that were significant in that language, and then in displaying the relations of equivalence that held between sentences of various types." [15] The basis of philosophy thus resides in the way one distinguishes significant from non-significant sentences in the language, and any criticism of Ayer, *et al.* must therefore be directed at this criterion of signification and at the typology which is distinguished.

Ayer makes a distinction between two and only two kinds of language convention or sentence usage, which he calls *analytic* and *synthetic* propositions. "A proposition is analytic when its validity depends solely on the definitions of the symbols it contains, and synthetic when its validity is determined by the facts of experience" (p. 62). We will deal with these one at a time. When a proposition is true (or false) solely because of the meaning of its component terms, then this is an analytic use of language called a *tautology*. To take Ayer's example, " 'Either some ants are parasitic or none are' is an analytic proposition. For one need not resort to observation to discover that there either are or are not ants which are parasitic. If one knows what is the function of the words 'either', 'or', and 'not', then one can see that any proposition of the form 'Either *p* is true or *p* is not true' is valid, independently of experience" (p. 79). An analytic proposition, then, says the same thing in different ways: "Water is H_2O", "6 times 2 is 12", etc. Such sentences are self-defining; their meaning is wholly contained in the language in which they are phrased. They tell us nothing about the outside world, but "although they give us no information about any empirical situation, they do enlighten us by illustrating the way in which we use certain symbols" (p. 79).

The world of the tautology, then, is totally linguistic. Attention is focused on the formal relationships of a sentence.

[15] *Op. cit.*, p. 62. Cf. the aims of transformational-generative grammar, p. 80 above. See Bibliography under Fodor and Katz.

Words of logic, such as *and, or, if, not, then, is,* are the basis of complex analytic propositions: "If X, then Y", "If X or Y, then not Z", etc. The equivalence between the parts of the proposition, seen in terms of sense-contents (for which see below), can be of two kinds: a logical truth, a meaningful proposition not a contradiction, and a logical falsehood, a contradiction. There is no empirical information in such sentences, but they are never meaningless: "We see, then, that there is a sense in which analytic propositions do give us new knowledge. They call attention to linguistic usages, of which we might otherwise not be conscious, and they reveal unsuspected implications in our assertions and beliefs. But we can see also that there is a sense in which they may be said to add nothing to our knowledge" (p. 80). Such tautologies, it is concluded, are the only satisfactory *a priori* propositions.

Analytic statements are not an end in themselves, however. They are an essential prelude to the more important statements called synthetic. Analytic statements say nothing factual; they rather prepare the formal ground and display the potential of the symbols that can be used in making statements of the synthetic type. These latter propositions assert facts. "The essential business of language is to assert or deny facts."[16] Such a sentence as "John is crying" or "It is starting to rain outside" can only have its validity (the common substitute for the word "truth" in these writings) judged by reference to observation, extra-linguistic data. The meaning is certainly not contained within the proposition, in the symbols. The total meaning resides in, and must be validated by, the facts of experience.

And it is at this point that logical positivism really links hands with Comte, Berkeley, the phenomenalists, and others. For if a synthetic statement is to be deemed valid (true), as would be the expected next philosophical step, then it must be verified. The criterion of a synthetic statement's validity is thus the mode of its verification: "The criterion which we use to test the genuineness of apparent statements of fact is the criterion of verificability. We say that a sentence is factually significant to any given person, if, and only if, he knows how to verify the propositions which it purports to express—that is, if he knows

---

[16] B. Russell, in the Introduction to Wittgenstein's *Tractatus.* See below for evidence for this statement's invalidity, p. 171.

what observations would lead him, under certain conditions, to accept the proposition as being true, or reject it as being false" (Ayer, p. 35). The meaning of an empirical proposition, Ayer goes on to say, cannot be *conclusively* verifiable. Conclusive or "strong" verification is only possible with analytic propositions, where the total meaning is within the very limited framework of the sentence. In the case of synthetic statements, it is only possible to have a probabilistic or "weak" verification. Scientific laws are no exception to this: any law is always based on past experience, and affirms a comparable state of affairs in the future; but it is nonetheless only a probability, because it is *logically* possible for the law not to hold. "No synthetic propositions are logically sacrosanct" (Ayer, p. 121). There are no *a priori* synthetic propositions—only *a posteriori*; and there is only a relative certainty in such propositions. Statements are more or less probable, depending on the tests which are relevant and available; and when no tests are available improbability becomes impossibility. The verifiability criterion is therefore used in its weak sense, which requires that only "some possible sense-experience should be relevant to the determination of their truth or falsehood". The corollary follows: if a sentence cannot be verified in this way, and it is not an analytic proposition, then it must be literally meaningless.

The criterion of meaningfulness is thus the mode of verification needed for any given statement, which in turn is based on what actual or possible sense-experiences are available, that can be used as tests in determined situations.[17] Any proposition which claims to be a fact (synthetic) and which fails to measure up to sense-evidence (or which is not able to be transformed into an equivalent sentence which can) is thus nonsense. Metaphysical utterances which cannot be verified are therefore meaningless and "all utterances about the nature of God are nonsensical" (p. 115). Metaphysics is satisfactorily eliminated: "Our charge against the metaphysician is not that he attempts to employ the understanding in a field where it cannot profitably venture, but that he produces sentences which fail to conform to the conditions under which alone a sentence can be literally significant" (p. 35). . . . "We may accordingly define a meta-

---

[17] The laboratory conditions are necessary, as will be seen from later arguments about mystical visions, and the like.

physical sentence as a sentence which purports to express a genuine proposition, but does, in fact, express neither a tautology nor an empirical hypothesis. And as tautologies and empirical hypotheses form the entire class of significant propositions, we are justified in concluding that all metaphysical assertions are nonsensical" (p. 41). The way is open for full-blooded materialism: "There is no field of experience which cannot, in principle, be brought under some form of scientific law, and no type of speculative knowledge about the world which is, in principle, beyond the power of science to give" (p. 48). Absolutes, universals, the traditional problems of philosophy are all dismissed. "The point which we wish to establish is that there cannot be any transcendent truths of religion. For the sentences which the theist uses to express such 'truths' are not literally significant" (pp. 117–18).

There is nothing left. If you do not speak analytically (and hence say next to nothing) or synthetically (in which case you are limited to a material world), or cannot substitute one proposition for another along the lines of logical equivalence,[18] then you have no further alternative in sense; all other language has no meaning apart from its sound, which has only aesthetic effect. It is emotional, senseless noise; pseudo-speculation; grammatical nonsense, for which criteria of truth or falsity do not even apply. And supernature is not the only criminal: the emotive theory of ethics and aesthetics makes the same criticism for these fields. To take one example: "This is wrong" has no verifiable norm, it is claimed. Its sole significance is as a display of the speaker's feeling, as if he had said "This!!" in a shocked tone of voice. Ethical problems are thus reduced to emotional overflows of feeling in words. As for the existence of God, and the "necessary" truths of theology, these are displayed as contradictions. Analytic and synthetic statements are mutually exclusive; but statements such as "the existence of God is necessary" claim to be both certain and to have empirical relevance, i.e., to be analytic and synthetic at the same time. If such statements claim to be factual, then, again by definition, they cannot be certain, because synthetic statements are at best probabilistic.

[18] Ayer, p. 70.

Other arguments for the existence of the supernatural are systematically attacked, and shown to be inadequate or meaningless when measured against the verification principle. For example, the argument from order in nature is condemned as insufficient: "no religious man would admit that this (regularity in nature) was all he intended to assert in asserting the existence of a god" (Ayer, p. 115). But if God is more than his manifestations, how can this "more" be defined? The divine attributes, without verification, remain labels with sound-value only.[19] What about mystical visions, then? Are these not evidence for a supernatural being? No, replies the positivist, because "in describing his vision the mystic does not give us any information about the external world; he merely gives us indirect information about the condition of his own mind" (p. 119). "Unless he can formulate his 'knowledge' in propositions that are empirically verifiable, we may be sure that he is deceiving himself" (p. 120). This reduction to the psychiatric level applies also to miracles or visions in public. For even if the positivist accepted such biblical events as miracles as being facts, and amenable to historical verification, he would still reject the theist argument, because the interpretation the Christian would put on these facts is not itself verifiable. Visual or aural or tactual sense-data take us so far, but no further; and it is always logically possible that as yet not understood natural phenomena are at work.

The subtlety of the attack is thus clear. The fact of theology is not disputed, but the theist's language—and a more sensitive part of a man it would be difficult to find! What more dangerous than saying "God does not exist" than to have "You are not even allowed to say—if you are intelligent—God does not exist". This, of course, hits at the agnostic and atheist also, because they accept the word "God" as meaningful, even if only to query or deny the validity of its referent. The illogicality behind all such uses, it is assumed, is in the attempt to frame

[19] Cf. R. Carnap, "The Elimination of Metaphysics": "In its *metaphysical* use . . . the word 'God' refers to something beyond experience. The word is deliberately divested of its reference to a physical being or to a spiritual being that is immanent in the physical. And as it is not given a new meaning, it becomes meaningless."

ideas about the infinite using finite language.[20] The only course left to people who want to believe in things metaphysical is silence! Religion is inexpressible; God is not to be found in language. Thus falls the whole of the rational basis of religion (that one assumes can be argued in words), the manifestations of a public liturgy and apostolate which require language, even private prayer.[21] There is no possibility of compromise between logical positivism and religion.

AN APPROACH TO A DEFENCE

The above précis has had to be selective in quotation, and by no means gives a complete picture of the reasoning behind the positivist conclusions; but enough has been said to characterize the positivist's main principles and provide data for counter-criticism. Ayer's book, as has already been said, is taken as one example of these views only (though probably the most influential). His views, in their early form, however, are typical of many others. More recently, he has modified and retracted certain statements (*vide* the Introduction to the 1960 Edition), but still supports the verification criterion as a useful tool and method of analysis. He admits, however, that it "suffers from a vagueness which it has not yet been found possible to eradicate. I doubt, however, if it is a wholly effective means of distinguishing questions of analysis or interpretation from questions of fact."[22] Earlier (1946), he had said, "although I should still defend the use of the criterion of verifiability as a methodological principle, I realize that for the effective elimination of metaphysics it needs to be supported by a detailed analyses of particular metaphysical arguments."[23] But why this fatal modification in principle?

The answer lies in the detailed and decisive criticism which the theory met with after Ayer's book was published. There have been published a number of approaches criticizing logical positivism as a whole and the total effect has been to remove

[20] Cf. Chapter X.
[21] See above, p. 149.
[22] Ayer, "Philosophy and Language", 1960 Inaugural lecture at Oxford, reprinted in *The Concept of a Person* (London, 1963), pp. 20–1.
[23] *Op. cit.*, p. 16. Such arguments have not yet appeared.

any attraction the theory ever had.[24] From the point of view of this book, I do not want to provide a summary of the range of arguments proposed elsewhere; rather to simply outline specifically linguistic objections to many of the issues. The general orientation for the criticism will be along the following lines: that the important underlying assumptions about the way language works are largely fallacious; that there is a prejudicial narrowness of definition about the use of terms, which makes any critique of metaphysical language thoroughly unreliable; and that the theory is not self-sufficient, but finds itself relying on extra-linguistic data to carry out its function.

Any linguist, especially one who has spent some time analysing spoken or written material collected together as a corpus, will affirm that it is not an easy matter to set up a model of classification to account for the range of forms in that data. Even in grammar (the most important part of a linguistic description, according to recent views) no two people are alike in the range of structures they use, and often a definite decision as to the nature of a given structure is not possible—one can only say that alternative forms are used, depending on a number of stylistic or contextual variables. It is not simply a question of "yes" or "no" in describing a language: usually it is a question of making judgements that have a "more-less" applicability.[25] Up to now, a reasonably simple and exhaustive formal description of the sentences of any style or register of English has not appeared. A semantic classification, of course, would be even more complex, as many more variables would be involved; and meaning is in any case a notoriously difficult concept to measure and classify. Such issues have already been discussed.[26] Language is flexible; its users are individuals, and proud of it, and its use is as varied as there are users.

To suggest, then, as does Ayer and others, that one can easily divide all meaningful sentences into two kinds of proposition, analytic and synthetic, and that one can ignore the difference between writing and speech,[27] is both naïve and a gross over-simplification of the language-using situation. With a little

[24] Cf. Bibliography under Ferré for further references.
[25] Cf. above, pp. 85, 102.
[26] Cf. above, Chapter VI under Grammar.
[27] Cf. Ayer, *op. cit.*, p. 62.

thought, many other kinds of sentence appear that could not be included under either heading, but which are certainly not meaningless. If propositions *state* facts or logical equivalences, then one is going to need a radical extension to the theory to account for the many types of question-pattern, whose main function is anything but statement. How do you verify "what time is it?", *as a question*? Again, there is the imperative function of language. A command does not state, and is hardly verifiable. But are all questions and commands then meaningless and emotive? A consideration of rhetorical questions or oaths would produce a similar problem. The performative function of language would also not be accounted for: "I hereby name this ship X", "I baptize thee John". Such activities cannot be verified because they only happen once. And there are also many statements, so phrased that they could never be verified by sense-data: "I wonder if he'll ever remember to say 'thank-you' ", "he may come to see us one day", etc.

Statistical studies quickly show that such sentences make up a large part of natural languages. They are largely a part of ordinary, routine conversation, where the concern is less for precision and more for adequacy in communication—if the message is "got across", that is all that matters. But such informal requests and replies occupy us more than we think in our day to day existence. Even when the user is a professional speaker, preacher or lecturer, a large part of one's daily verbal output is informal "chat". Narrative or precise descriptive statement is relatively exceptional. Language's main purpose is intelligible communication, but there are many kinds of communication, many uses of language,[28] and a precise, specialized use is only one. Just as common is quite the opposite use, where language is used more for the sake of its sound than its content, and is still not meaningless. This is the phenomenon that the anthropologist Malinowski called "phatic communion", "language used in free, aimless, social intercourse".[29] It covers the everyday conversation "about nothing", empty catch-phrases, polite remarks about the weather and the like, opening gambits in greeting. But the fact that much of this language is highly

[28] See above, Chapter VIII.
[29] See the supplement to *The Meaning of Meaning*, pp. 313–14; also Quirk, *op. cit.*, pp. 44, ff.

conventionalized, often semi-unconscious (do you remember how many times you say "hello" in a day?) does not mean that this language is meaningless. It has its proper function, usually as a prelude to further communication; it is an important part of getting and maintaining the right atmosphere.[30]

Ayer's proposal to take analytic and synthetic statements as a norm or measuring-rod for language thus disregards too much of the rest of language to be valid. The logical positivist claims the support of common sense, and, as we shall see, relies on the principle that the meaning of language resides in its use; but his linguistic analysis is by no means a common-sense one, and the man in the street would certainly protest with vigour if told that his request for a cup of tea was meaningless. Analytic and synthetic statements are not, then, to be taken as the characteristic meaning-carriers for language, because the primary function of language is not to inform, in the sense of "add to our knowledge of the external world"; the primary function of language is to communicate, and one can only judge the validity of a linguistic communication with reference to the context which stimulated it.

There is a further point. Linguistic contexts are not better or worse—only different. While Ayer is mistaken in assuming that the functional norm of English is constituted by analytic and synthetic propositions, for any norm that can be determined statistically, it is still unjustifiable to *evaluate* other kinds of language against it. "Better" and "worse", "more meaningful" and "less meaningful" are terms which are inapplicable outside of defined contexts. To state otherwise is to return to the old views (still, unfortunately, current) about linguistic correctness: that there is one kind of language which is somehow better, purer, more meaningful than other kinds, and should be the one taught in schools. Earlier chapters have shown how this view can be traced from Classical times. It is nonetheless illegitimate; and the importance of context in making decisions about usage is gradually being realized. A linguistic standard is based on the suitability of language forms to a situation: pulpit language for the pulpit, public-house language for the pub, mathematical

---

[30] Cf. the deliberate use of sound for aesthetic purposes—alliteration, assonance and rhyme in literature, for example—where again there is a positive communicative function.

language for talk about mathematics, and theological language for talk about God. This kind of linguistic conformity is the only kind of genuine correctness; talk about arbiters for a language as a whole is misplaced.

And so, to take one kind of language—call it "logical" language—and define it by reference to analytic and synthetic propositions, this is reasonable; but to use it as an arbitrary measuring-rod for other kinds of language, condemning them for not fitting its mould, is highly unreasonable. If theological language (or, more generally, the language of metaphysics) does not fit the patterns of non-theological or (in our case) logical positivist language, this then does not validate a dismissal of the former as being "of unsound mind". For logical positivism to do so is but another example of the regrettably naïve parochiality that has been typical of amateur statements about language for many years.[31]

Some specific misorientations come to mind immediately. Terms from different and incompatible situational languages (or registers) are made equivalent, whereas the fundamental differences in their respective contexts of situation make such forced synonymity quite illegitimate. In all probability, a technical term in theology is going to have a quite different range of application (meaning) if used as a technical term in some other discipline. But positivism does not hesitate to equate, for example, the normal, informal use of the term "necessity" with the highly specialized use of the term in theological statement. On another page, "incomprehensible" (of God) is equated with "insignificant"—perhaps an illogical equation in any context. What such procedures amount to is a narrowness of definition, whereby the full range of meanings for crucial, polysemantic terms is ignored, and only those meanings which accord well with positivist doctrine are included in the argument. For example, why should the only valid kind of "explanation" be of the scientific or logical kind? Intuitive explanation exists, to name but one other. And non-scientific, or common-sense explanations can still be meaningful.

But in any case, it is more than likely that the interpretation of a word in theological context is going to be very different

[31] Cf. above, p. 114.

from an interpretation of the same word in, say, the context of physics, because the logic of the two languages is different, and the kind of facts dealt with by both are so dissimilar.[32] It is clear, for example, that metaphysics deals in abstract words more thoroughly than most other departments of knowledge and it has been seen how abstract language is the area of language most prone to vagueness and different interpretations:[33] but occasional vagueness does not exclude the possibility of precision, and conflicting interpretations do not necessarily imply meaninglessness. The language of theology, for example, or the statements of traditional Christianity are self-contained and have their own logic—a logic which, incidentally, may at times be similar to that of positivist analytic method, e.g. "the statements of traditional Christianity strictly imply certain historical statements, and certain statements about the ultimate fate of men; they are incompatible with the contraries of these statements."[34] But to understand fully the logic of the statements of Christianity, some addition to normal synchronic description and analytic statement is needed, for one needs to provide the totality of historical perspective which gives such statements their force and meaning. The popular term "charged with meaning" is often applied to such statements, referring to those connotations which derive from an awareness of the function the statements have had in the history of the Church, particularly in its first days.[35] This is the main reason, then, why it would not be legitimate to equate in usage "Jehovah is angry" with "it is thundering",[36] because "Jehovah" in this respect has taken on a certain amount of traditional meaning in this way which is completely lacking with such an unemotional phrase as "it is thundering".

More important in determining the logic of these statements and terminology is an understanding of the position the term

---

[32] See the discussion by C. Hartshorne, *Downside Review*, 247 (1958–1959); and L. Williams, *Downside Review*, 237 (1956), pp. 191 ff., where the theologian's "blik" is discussed in detail.

[33] Cf. pp. 49, 104.

[34] H. Meynell, *Sense, Nonsense and Christianity* (London and New York, 1964), p. 247.

[35] Cf. above, p. 100 on removed situational context.

[36] Ayer, *op. cit.*, p. 116.

"God" has in relation to such statements. It will be found that, in theological language in particular, it is a logical cornerstone, from which all other terms derive their full meaning. Words like "truth", "creative", "merciful" and "love" in the language of theology must be interpreted carefully with an eye to this relationship. The word "happiness", for example, is going to have a very different definition according as to whether one believes in an afterlife or not; and the same kind of reasoning applies for any other terminology which implies a sense of values. It is not my concern to give a detailed treatment of the logic of metaphysical language here,[37] but a few examples of the kind of problem posed will be relevant. At the grammatical level, for instance, "God made man" and "Michael made a sand-castle" are very similar; but the logic of their respective contexts puts them worlds apart. Similarly with "God loves you". Again, a sentence like "Where was God before the universe was made?" is meaningless in metaphysical logic, because words from a register for which terms of time and space ("where", "before") are meaningful are placed in the same structure along with a word from a different register ("God") for which such terms have no meaning. Indeed, how far can one legitimately use tenses to talk about God at all, because all tenses imply time? But such problems have already been discussed.[38] Finally, at the lexical level, one can ask such helpful questions as what "nothing" means in the sentence "God created the world out of nothing", or of "son" in "Son of Man", "Son of God", and "son of our butcher", or of the implication of attributing "personality" to the deity.[39]

Meynell, in his book, discusses some of the possible verification procedures that could be used in verifying the statements of traditional Christianity. The statements made are certainly less obviously precise and less easily verifiable than, say, scien-

[37] For an approach to which, see Meynell, *op. cit.*; and the approach suggested by Ferré, *op. cit.* Cf. also, J. L. Moreau, *Language and Religious Language* (Philadelphia, 1960), p. 105: "We shall have to view the theological vocabulary as a structural semantic system within which there is operative a specific way of organizing and previsioning experience."

[38] Cf. above, Chapter X.

[39] Another kind of logic, based on the relevance of private facts, is discussed below.

tific statements; but it is still possible to say something about them. For example, some, though not all, of a mystery's truth-conditions can be satisfied. Miracles and visions, for instance, must be defined carefully before the definition is allowed to be put forward for linguistic analysis. A miracle (following Augustine) is a striking exception to the normal course of events (*not*, an exception to nature, which merely adds a difficulty), but there are certain requirements which the miracle must conform to imposed by the logic of Christianity. The state of affairs or human agent to which the event draws attention should be consistent with an already accepted pattern of divine revelation (p. 198). A miracle has therefore two possible verification procedures: it must not violate the traditionally accepted pattern of miracles, and it must fit in with and be of relevance to the Christian framework of beliefs. Thus, a vision talking about soapflakes would hardly qualify as relevant, and a vision saying God does not exist would be excluded from acceptance on the grounds of inconsistency.[40] Again, one would not expect to hear bad language or abuse of the Pope in a visitation by the mother of God. "The ultimate validation of a vision is part of the validation of the whole religious system in relation to which it occurs."[41]

Moreover, if meaning is ultimately determined by use, and use resides in the users,[42] then the beliefs of the users are obviously going to be an important part of the total context which must be considered before language can be assessed. The social, personal and historical backgrounds are all-important. Thus "The king is dead; long live the king" is only an apparent contradiction, as long as we are aware of the conventions. Why then should verificational analysis make theological paradoxes contradictions in terms? To the positivist, paradoxes are examples of linguistic confusion, but to poets, theists, proverb-users and many other "ordinary" people, paradoxes are not meaningless, but are rather attempts to phrase a higher or more fundamental mean-

---

[40] Which is not to deny the possibility of visions from ungodly sources; merely that such statements as these visions produced would not be utilized as evidence in any discussion of the nature of Christianity.

[41] Meynell, *op. cit.*, p. 210.

[42] Cf. above, p. 101.

ing, that ordinary language cannot express.[43] "Bitter-sweet" is not meaningless; it has a vivid and intensifying function, which can only be comprehended by concentrating on the component lexical items in the context. Paradox must be taken seriously, especially when the paradox concerns such matters as how the existence of both good and evil do not make a contradiction out of God. It is not enough to say that the two words are irreconcilable in the same context if one has not paid close attention to the full use of both terms in that context; for in religious contexts, one would find that the collocations of "good" and "evil" are very different from what one gets else-where—and the collocation is an important part of the total meaning.[44] In religious discussions, "good" and "suffering" can go together (collocate), as do "pleasure" and "evil" in many contexts. And the Christian looking outwards from his faith must be prepared to find similar reversals in meaning from what he is used to. A large part of ecumenism is getting to know the other side's language: and in the last analysis, it is detailed information like this which is of importance.

Which brings us to the most important terminological objection of all: the positivist use of the word "fact". Empirical facts are assumed to be the only kind of facts, and the only valid knowledge, it is claimed, is that based on empirical observation and derived from the senses. But it is commonly accepted that there is non-sensory knowledge as well as sensory, and hence that there are also two kinds of facts, non-sensory and sensory. Sensory facts are catered for (although inadequately) by the positivist analytic and synthetic propositions; but non-sensory analytic propositions are dismissed as tautologous, and its synthetic propositions are classed as meaningless. It is impossible, in Ayer's view, to base a deductive system of philosophy on

[43] Cf. J. Wisdom, "Philosophical Perplexity", *Philosophy and Psycho-Analysis*, p. 50: "I wish to represent them as also symptoms of linguistic penetration".

[44] Cf. above, p. 88. Meynell makes the point that religious statements about the Trinity are similar to those about relativity, in that they relate to the use of the language system as a whole, rather than to particular parts of it; they are "regulative principles to the manipulation of the conceptual scheme within which they occur" (p. 175). Catholic beliefs are thus either in accordance with or in contradiction to these basic formulae.

intuitively perceived truths, first principles. The narrowness in this definition of the term "fact" becomes clear when one considers just what other kinds of knowledge exist that are equally valid, the private facts, as opposed to the public ones. Language is not given meaning solely by reference to the latter.

Private facts cannot all be translated without remainder into public language—one reason being that it is impossible to determine rules of logical equivalence that would hold between statements of the two kinds. There may be a strong connection between our observable behaviour and our private facts, but this is not a necessary one. For example, I am directly conscious of whether I am in pain or not, but I need not show it. Belief that "God exists", as a statement of private fact, is also logically unprovable. But there are many kinds of knowledge, commonly accepted as such, that one could classify as non-sensory derived private facts which one could put into language. Cognition would necessarily include the following, for example: mental decisions, arrived at by introspection, about moral issues, for instance—mental "battles"; the fact of conscience, which may often be viewed indirectly via behaviour, but which may also function unobserved save by its owner; introspection about public facts—mental arithmetic, brain-teasers, and the like; the internal experience of remembering, usually a linguistic business, which can produce extra knowledge ("flashes of light"), or of deliberation before or during a game such as chess; the mental movements of daydreams and aesthetic effects—one can be "moved" visibly, but also invisibly, when one "doesn't show" feeling; the intellectual inspiration (νοῦς) or non-sensory knowing which produces commitment to a course of action—what R. M. Hare has called a "blik"; and there is even scientific data which needs an internal interpretation of conflicting sense-data to be understood and resolved, e.g. the curved stick entering water—for which matter, the objectivity of science, machine analysis, the computer, and so on, is likewise only relative, its value depending on the interpretative faculties of the research worker.[45]

There is thus a wealth of material which could be grouped under the heading of non-sensory knowing. To it could be

[45] Cf. above, pp. 48, 75.

added historical facts, which are not immediately available to sense-experience (only the historical book or record is),[46] and Joad's piece of one-upmanship: "scientific knowledge entails the existence of one fact which is not an empirical fact, the fact, namely, that the events in our minds are also a knowledge of empirical facts".[47]

Now whether one calls the above private facts "facts" or not, it is clear that one can still make statements about such events, and that such statements are meaningful to oneself and to others outside of oneself.[48] Once again it is emphasized that precision is not the sole criterion of meaningfulness: one can be meaningful and imprecise, even empirically. The wider, the more general or abstract one's purpose becomes, the more imprecise statements tend to be. This is only to be expected. No one would expect language used about God to be as clear as language about physics, or the language of physics as clear as a novel. Not only are there different kinds of complexity involved, but the assessment of difficulty is itself impossible to generalize about, difficulty in linguistic matters being largely based on one's familiarity with the particular mode of discourse used. Chemical formulae are meaningless to Mr A. because he is not a chemist and cannot talk chemists' "language". But chemical formulae are not therefore meaningless. Just such an argument applies to the positivist's use of theological statements.

To summarize the argument so far: The primary criticism is levelled at the making of value-judgements in absolute terms about incompatible kinds of language, so that style A is made to take precedence over style B: this approach to language I would call naïve and egocentric. The assumption that such comparisons can take place at all is itself invalid. Equally invalid is the conclusion that of all "languages" available, the positivist type is the norm of meaningfulness. This is dogma without reason. The positivist procedure is also criticizable.

[46] If historical facts are verifiable only "in principle", like events far away in space (Cf. Ayer, *op. cit.*, p. 19), then this is getting very near to setting up universal criteria of the kind he explicitly rejects.

[47] *Op. cit.*, p. 77.

[48] Cf. Meynell, *op. cit.*: "Statements of private fact seem to occupy, as it were, a logical space of their own—that is to say, they are neither implied by nor incompatible with any statement about the material world" (p. 37).

Their analysis of language into propositions is inadequate and misleading, as is the criterion for such propositions, verification of sense-contents. There are also meanings one cannot satisfactorily express,[49] a common theme of many poets and authors, struggling to put their feelings into words. "If I could only find words to express . . ." is, after all, almost a cliché. There *are* things which cannot be expressed satisfactorily (God being one), but it does not follow that what cannot be expressed is nothing at all. And "Philosophers should be continually trying to say what cannot be said".[50]

There is a further point concerning the narrowness of the procedure, which is connected with the positivist theory of meaning. Wittgenstein, in *The Blue Book*, differs from positivist thought in this, as in so many matters. He suggests that one source of philosophical confusion is "the tendency to look for something in common to all the entities which we commonly subsume under a general term". Such a theory would imply that there is a common element present every time a word (or set of words) is used, which is the key meaning of that word or phrase; that every time the word "dog" is used, for example, there is a fundamentally similar referent present. But this theory only holds for some relatively simple polysemantic cases; it is very fallacious for words of great complexity, especially abstract words.

It is not the case that there *must* be something in common, but rather that the words are *related* to each other in certain differing ways (cf. *Phil. Inv.*, 65 ff.). The positivist view assumed the contrary, however. It claimed that sense-experience was the common factor behind all verifiable propositions, and that therefore meaning was to be equated with the mode of verification, which was equated with sense-experience. The main objection to this theory is its disregard for context: meaning does not exist in a vacuum. And, as Fr A. Kenny says

[49] Cf. Wittgenstein's ladder analogy below, p. 185; and *Tractatus*, 4. 1212: "What *can* be shown, *cannot* be said".

[50] Wisdom, *Philosophy and Psycho-Analysis*, p. 50. It also follows that unsayable experiences should not be measured by solely linguistic criteria; if one does so measure them, they will naturally be dismissed as meaningless. Cf. above, Chapter X.

in his discussion of this, which he calls the Highest Common Factor (HCF) theory of meaning:

> It might be called the spirits-and-water fallacy, after the well-known story of the scientists who were investigating the causes of drunkenness. These scientists, having drunk first whisky and water, then brandy and water, and then rum and water, and having found that on each occasion intoxication ensued, decided that the cause of drunkenness must be water, since it alone was present in all three occasions. A similar fallacy is committed by those who say that because sense-experience is the one element common to all instances of verification, the real meaning of "verification" is sense-experience.[51]

It would appear, then, that verificational analysis is much too narrow to be set up as an answer to the accumulated wisdom of generations. Its status as a philosophic system is seriously undermined by its inadequacy. It is, in fact, one kind of analytical device for one kind of language, no more: "What we have here, then, is not really a criterion of meaningfulness (a way of separating wheat from chaff) but a criterion of empiricality (a way, as we might say, of separating wheat from oats, or barley, or rice)".[52] Any theory of meaning must first and foremost be exhaustive, accounting for *all* linguistic usages (or language "games"—Wittgenstein) of a speech community. Such a theory would then examine the verification critique as an attempt to account for a certain part of the data, and go on to examine the rest, which verification did not (could not) account for. The verificational principle is not itself such a theory. Ferré emphasizes this point, and brings the positivist position to a logical conclusion:

> The verification principle may be of considerable usefulness in many contexts, but it is utterly misunderstood if it is taken as "the" criterion for judging the meaningfulness of all language. An embarrassing example of an assertion which is not meaningful when tested by the verification principle is—the verification principle itself! The statement that the meaning of any proposition will be found either in verbal rules (if the proposition is

[51] "Aquinas and Wittgenstein", *Downside Review*, 249 (1959), p. 224.
[52] R. M. Hare, "Religion and Morals", *Faith and Logic*, ed. B. Mitchell (London, 1957), p. 177. Cf. 1 Cor. 12. 20–1, "There are indeed many members, yet but one body...."

182   LANGUAGE AND LOGICAL POSITIVISM

analytic) or in equivalent statements referring to actual or possible sense-experiences (if the proposition is synthetic) seems to be asserting a fact, not offering a definition or a rule of usage. But if the verification principle is not itself analytic, what actual or possible sense-experiences could be relevant to its verification or falsification? No such experience will even in principle be relevant to the task! ... On the basis of the verification principle, therefore, the verification principle is devoid of meaning![53]

Ayer, in the 1946 Introduction, attempted to forestall this reasoning by asserting that the verificational principle is a tautology: "I wish the principle of verification itself to be regarded, not as an empirical hypothesis, but as a definition" (p. 16). But this too has unfortunate results. If it is a tautology, then we are only "juggling with the meaning of words", and this "cannot solve empirical problems" (p. 96). But the verification principle *does* make empirical statements, and has as its main purpose the very empirical business of clarification. Moreover, "from a set of tautologies, taken by themselves, only further tautologies can be validly deduced". If Ayer maintains this position, then logical positivism becomes pointless. To be treated seriously, positivism *must* claim more scope; but as soon as it does, then it becomes just another philosophic principle, on a par with other philosophies telling us about objects in the outside world, and is open to the above objections. Judged by its own terms, to state that metaphysical propositions are meaningless is itself meaningless. Joad goes so far as to call the verification principle a metaphysical statement![54]

When one considers such points, it is hard to understand the frequently heard positivist remark, that "the philosopher has no right to despise the beliefs of common sense". On the face of it, common sense would seem to be being despised all the time. Who uses language solely in terms of analytic and synthetic propositions? How can one maintain that experience consists wholly of observable sense-contents? Even granting a definition of "experience" as "sensory experience", there are still problems. "Sense-contents" are defined vaguely by Ayer as "the

[53] Ferré, *op. cit.*, p. 53. Cf. Joad, *op. cit.*, p. 66, for the same point arrived at from a different angle.
[54] *Op. cit.*, p. 71.

immediate data not merely of 'outer' but also of 'introspective' sensation" (p. 53). They are given a linguistic (not an onto-logical) status to avoid the charge of being themselves meta-physical—though whether this can be defended is another question. But it is not true to say that material things can be analysed without remainder into these sense-contents, or sensa-tions of perception. If I say "this is a boy", it cannot merely be equated with the sentence "I am having a sense experience to which the word 'boy' can apply"—even if people thought like this anyway. There is more to the first sentence, for it also implies that there *is* a boy who is the cause of the sense-experiences I am having. Sense-contents require a place of origin which, it would seem, is of greater importance philo-sophically than the intermediary sense-content.

Why introduce sense-contents at all, then? They have to be, because if such information about origins is not excluded, the positivist theory loses its individualistic status as a dealer in language matters only: once again, it would become just another philosophy, which discusses the legitimacy and classification of things in the public and private worlds, the very thing the posi-tivist is reacting against.[55] The situation is difficult, therefore. He wishes to exclude all considerations which deal with the non-linguistic basis of things, but such considerations are con-tinually being forced upon him, and he finds himself talking about the world behind the sense-contents. Language is a social fact; it is used to refer to things and events in the real world, private and public; it cannot be discussed sensibly by abstract-ing it from its social context; and any linguistic philosophy is going to be continually brought back to this social context, which lies behind the sense-contents. Verification is shaky ground. How does one know when a verification is exhaustive without knowing the meaning of the proposition one is trying to verify independently? How can one avoid an infinite re-gression in its use? "This is a boy" is expressible as certain sense-contents which either are occurring or could occur. But this is an empirical statement. It is therefore verifiable. It can

[55] Ayer denies being a solipsist. But it is difficult to see how a solipsistic position is avoided if the theory of sense-contents is main-tained. Any statement Ayer makes about the world must be solely in terms of sense-contents; but sense-contents are private to the percipient.

therefore be expressed in other sense-contents which either are occurring or could occur. But this is an empirical statement. . . .

The self-contradictory nature of much of this philosophy is thus apparent in many ways: the meaninglessness of the criterion of meaningfulness; the appeal to a common-sense which is not common; the discussion of the illegitimate status of physical objects using words, which are physical objects, and given legitimate status; the impossibility of certain propositions, which is itself a certain proposition;[56] and so on. Logical positivism does not provide a solution, if a solution is an explanation of things which satisfies other experts in the field. There have been insufficient results for this to happen. The old problems of philosophy may disappear—but "they disappear not because they have been solved but because they are dismissed."[57] The many modifications to original views have reflected the insecurity. Ayer admitted in 1946, for example, that there was only one proper sense of the word "meaning" that the verification principle applied to, and allowed that metaphysical statements may have meaning in one of these other senses; and more recently: "the metaphysician is treated no longer as a criminal but as a patient: there may be good reasons why he says the strange things that he does".[58] But this is academic egotism.

So that if logical positivism's only positive recommendation is that philosophy ought to concentrate on one kind of meaning only (i.e. logical positivist meaning) and ignore all other usages, its naïvety is clear. There remains, however, some necessary comments on the positivist view of usage, which conflicts in certain important respects with the linguist's view.

Wittgenstein's doctrine, "The meaning of a word is its use", was one of the stimuli for the positivist position. But the positivists differed from the Wittgensteinian philosophy in trying to restrict the scope of philosophy to linguistic decisions. Its phenomenalism is the nearest we are ever allowed to get,

[56] Ayer in the 1946 Introduction retracted his denial that there were certain propositions, and allowed in ostensive propositions (those which directly record an immediate experience, e.g. "This is blue") as certain, not just probable. But the above statement is not of this kind.

[57] Joad, op. cit., p. 22.

[58] Ayer, ed. Logical Positivism, Intro., p. 8 (New York, 1959). Cf. above, p. 169.

officially, to the real world; objects are reduced to the status of sense-contents.[59] But Wittgenstein had no such preoccupation with linguistic judgements: his work is as much about the world as about language. The concentration on language was an essential part of his attempt to do away with "the customary traffic in philosophic generalities" and to return to individual cases ("Every proposition has its own logic"), but it was only a means to a higher end, which Wittgenstein himself was hard put to express. To reach his final position, one would have to forget the train of reasoning that led there: such a person "must so to speak throw away the ladder, after he has climbed up on it".[60]

This is a very different kind of linguistic philosophy from the positivists', then, which tries, albeit inconsistently, to leave out the world completely. If it had succeeded in doing this, of course, it would have hurt no one: verbal discussion is indeed a useful tool of clarification. But Ayer's book does not limit itself to intralinguistic judgements of the kind he proposes to make. On the contrary, it incorporates many non-linguistic statements, value-judgements. It is hard to see, indeed, how a philosophy which claimed to reside *wholly* in language could be a philosophy at all, but a linguistics—and a remedial or corrective linguistics at that, not a constructive one.[61] The recommendations of such a "philosophy" would not be allowed to enter into questions of empirical meaning without taking whole contexts into consideration, because this would be bad linguistics; but once contextual considerations come in, one is well and truly embedded in affairs of the world, and the philosophy would be immediately inconsistent.

The philosopher *is* concerned with analysing the true meaning of statements, but this can only be done by considering the facts that are involved over and above the linguistic framework which refers to them. Russell has also commented that analysis cannot be identified with linguistic activity alone: he says that it is only possible within a limited field "to treat language as an independent realm, which can be studied without regard to non-linguistic occurrences". Philosophy may well be called a

---

[59] Cf. E. Gellner, *Words and Things* (London, 1959), p. 18: "Logical positivism is radical empiricism formulated as a doctrine about language and meaning".

[60] *Tractatus* 6. 54.   [61] Cf. Chapters V, VI.

matter of clarification, but it is not *just* a matter of words, talk about talk. But even if one allows the positivist to have recourse to those elements of context (immediate operations) that are relevant to determine the mode of verification—though he would need a separate set of procedures to be able to isolate them—what then? It could then be argued that if "meaning is in use", then religious assertions have meaning because they are used. To this, the positivist could retort that there is an ambiguity in "use" here: no one would deny that such assertions are used (in the sense "are employed"); but many would deny that they have a use (in the sense "have a valid function"). However, this answer is still too permissive and solves no problems on either side. If meaning is use, then all uses have meaning; but all religions, philosophies, sects (and atheism) use language, therefore all have meaning—a trivial conclusion. To decide upon the validity of different uses, which is more important, recourse *must* be had to extra-linguistic philosophical criteria, and this puts us back where we started before logical positivism arrived. We need the perspective of a more abstract philosophic system or a divinely inspired authority. It has, after all, long been appreciated that usage cannot settle normative issues as to how we *ought* to think (the naturalistic fallacy), and P. T. Geach argues that as language is one facet only of *Weltanschauung*, differences between world-views cannot be sorted out by linguistic analysis alone.[62]

Philosophy, then, cannot be restricted solely to linguistics: larger issues are involved all the time. Thus, while positivist linguistics is at variance with the views of most modern linguists, it is also at variance with itself; for while claiming to deal in common sense and to be based on language in ordinary use, it does not consistently maintain this position. Its therapeutic aim, to *correct* "errors" arising from "misuse" of ordinary language (which uses phrases like "this is bad" or "God is good") is not consistent with the maxim that usage is the guide.[63] And as soon as the positivist restricts usage to one

---

[62] Supplement 25, *Proceedings of the Aristotelian Society*. Similarly, questions of the validity of different questions of interpretation in art, belief, etc., can only be resolved by extra-linguistic criteria.

[63] Gellner, *op. cit.*, p. 20, calls linguistic philosophy a "Night Watchman theory of philosophy", in that its function is to be ever guarding

kind of usage, as he then must, major linguistic criticisms can be directed at him. It is the reversal of the true position. The very ordinary language which uses terms like "God" and "good" reasonably coherently is the norm; specialist (i.e. philosophers') language is not.[64] But the positivist, as we have seen, is continually giving important terms a meaning that suits his own position, but which is not in accordance with the view of the body of people who have to use the term. They, the originators of their kind of language, are criticized for not using language in a positivist way.[65]

There are other linguistic criticisms that can be levelled at this procedure. These days, logical judgements are brought into language at every level, and though some have their uses, they must not be made the criterion to which speakers must conform. "Each proposition has its own logic" must always be borne in mind. And this logic is derived from the total social context in which the proposition is and has been used. There is no single logic for the whole of language. Many propositions have a similar logic in common—this would be essential if we were to communicate at all, and the existence of *langue* shows that within one language there *are* universals of organization. But while the positivist claims to be making statements about *langue*, all he is doing in fact is making statements about one register of *langue*, and a very specialized section at that, which happens to have had its logic more precisely defined than others.

It is thus quite in order to make generalizations about language, so long as one bears in mind which part of language one is referring to. It is also quite in order to utilize an operational theory of meaning, so long as one realizes that not all meaning resides in uses that are empirically observable: the facts of interpretation, feeling, and the like, must be considered. And one can criticize other points in the positivist linguistic reasoning. The definition of a proposition as a "unit of mean-

---

against possible abuse, which is inherent in language. But cf. Wittgenstein's decision: "Philosophy may in no way interfere with the actual use of language, it can in the end only describe it" (*Phil. Inv.*, 124).

[64] There is a case for saying that "standard language is essentially theistic", C. Hartshorne, *Downside Review*, 247, p. 8.

[65] Cf. above, p. 103.

ing" is too reminiscent of other semantically-based definitions
to be satisfactory. The criterion of meaning is again implied in
the notion of logical equivalence, which is taken for granted as
possible, but there is no indication as to how comparison of
meanings is to take place: how does one measure meaning?[66]
Thirdly, there is an unempirical reliance on sentence division of
the subject/predicate kind, which excludes from study the many
"verbless" constructions ("yes", "no", "thank you", etc.) which
are meaningful. Fourthly, the positivist function is over-rated;
not all language needs clarification; error is not inherent in language, only at times in its users. To make the pathological state
the norm is a distortion: communication does break down, but
only occasionally. Further, when one is talking about language in
use, it is unrealistic to rely on the actual language uttered for
the total meaning communicated; a large part of the information in a message derives from context, which has to be "read
in" to language. And from another point of view, much of what
we say is unnecessary (redundant) anyway.[67] Language does not
exist in a vacuum, and must not be studied as if it did.

Finally, there is the important criticism that Ayer in his
book, and logical positivists in general, restrict themselves to
one language family for all their statements, Indo-European,
and their philosophy, as a result, is largely governed by the
bias of these languages—not by universal laws of thought. This
is not to deny the presence of *some* useful generalization, of
course. The positivist claim that philosophers have been taken
in by the structure of their language[68] has certainly been in
evidence at times, and it is defensible that there are "poverties"
(in the sense of "gaps") in language that should be made good
(Ayer, p. 67); again, in their attempt at clarification, the positivists do at least partly succeed in revealing "what may be
called the structure of the language in question" (p. 62). But the
majority of decisions and descriptions they arrive at, it must be
emphasized, are limited in application to the specific registers of
specific groups of languages that display roughly similar structures—a very dissatisfying basis for a philosophical theory

[66] Cf. Bibliography under Osgood. The question of synonymity has
been discussed in Chapters VI and VII.
[67] Cf. above, p. 78.
[68] Ayer, *op. cit.*, p. 51, for example.

which claims to have some kind of universal validity. There are many languages in the world, for example, for which terminology like subject/predicate, and so on, is irrelevant. In such cases, how can positivist analysis even begin? And from another point of view, if all problems reside in language, then different languages are going to bring different problems and different views of the same problem. Is it then going to be a question of one language or language-group having a clearer solution to conceptual discussion than another?

At least one moral is clear. Usage is important, but it must be carefully watched. To take the Oxford English Dictionary as a kind of holy Writ is only permissible if its limitations are kept in mind. Language (and hence norms) change continuously, but dictionaries have supplements only at long intervals. Similarly, any belief relying wholly on language can have no claim to permanence. Semantic change is normal, and if one is logomorphically inclined (i.e. seeing the world solely through the forms of language), then one's beliefs are going to vary from time to time—not a very satisfying intellectual position! To take language as one's ultimate criterion of reality is not good, because language is not a good reflector. It makes divisions where none really exist (the colour spectrum, body-mind dualisms); it refers to facts that are not observationally verifiable, and its forms change with time. It is quite helpful to look on language as a kind of indispensable tool, which many scholars, Christian and otherwise, would do well to understand better. To make it a fundamental criterion for living, however, is to get one's priorities wrong. Language makes a good servant, but it is a bad master.

SELECT BIBLIOGRAPHY

In this series:
AUVRAY, Paul, POULAIN, Pierre, and BLAISE, Albert: *Sacred Languages.*

ALLEN, W. S.: "Ancient ideas on the origin and development of language", *Transactions of the Philological Society*, Oxford, Blackwell, 1948.

BACH, E.: *An Introduction to Transformation Grammars*, New York, Holt, 1964.

BOUYER, L.: *Rite and Man: Natural Sacredness and Christian Liturgy*, Notre Dame, Ind., University of Notre Dame Press, and London, Burns and Oates, 1963.

CUNLIFFE, C. (Editor): *English in the Liturgy*, London, Burns and Oates, 1961.

DODD, C. H.: *The Interpretation of the Fourth Gospel*, Cambridge and New York, Cambridge Univ. Press, 1953.

FERRE, F.: *Language, Logic and God*, London, Eyre and Spottiswoode, and New York, Harper, 1962.

FODOR, J., and KATZ, J. (Editors): *The Structure of Language: Readings in the Philosophy of Language*, Englewood Cliffs, N. J., Prentice-Hall, 1964.

FRIES, C. C.: *The Structure of English*, New York, Harcourt Brace, 1952.

GIMSON, A. C.: *An Introduction to the Pronunciation of English*, London, Arnold, 1962.

HALL, R. A.: *Linguistics and Your Language*, New York, Doubleday, 1960.

HALLIDAY, M. A. K., McINTOSH, A., and STREVENS, J.: *The Linguistic Sciences and Language Teaching*, London, Longmans, 1964.

HAYAKAWA, S. I.: *Language in Thought and Action*, London, Allen and Unwin, 1952, and New York, Harcourt, 1949.

JESPERSON, O.: *Language: Its Nature, Development and Origin*, New York, Macmillan, 1949, and London, Allen and Unwin; *Mankind, Nations and Individual*, London, Allen and Unwin, 1946.

JONES, A.: *God's Living Word*, London, Geoffrey Chapman, and New York, Sheed and Ward, 1961.

KORZYBSKI, A.: *Science and Sanity*, Lakeville, Conn., Inst. of Gen. Semantics, 1958.

KÜNG, H.: *The Living Church*, London and New York, Sheed and Ward, 1961.

LADEFOGED, P.: *Elements of Acoustic Phonetics*, Edinburgh, Oliver and Boyd, and Chicago, Univ. of Chicago Press, 1962.

LEHMANN, W. P.: *Historical Linguistics: An Introduction*, New York, Holt, 1963.

LEVIE, J.: *The Bible: Word of God in Words of Men*, London, Geoffrey Chapman, and New York, Kenedy, 1961.

LYONS, J.: *Structural Semantics*, Special Publication of the Philological Society, Oxford, Blackwell, 1964.

MALMBERG, B.: *Phonetics*, New York, Dover Publications, 1963: *Structural Linguistics and Human Communication*, New York, Academic Press, 1963.

McGLYNN, J. V.: "Philosophy and Analysis", *Downside Review*, 250–1 (1959–60).

MORRIS, C.: *Signs, Language and Behaviour*, Englewood Cliffs, N. J., Prentice-Hall, 1946.

OGDEN, C. K.: "Word Magic", *Psyche*, 18 (1952); with RICHARDS, I. A.: *The Meaning of Meaning*, London, Routledge and Kegan Paul, 1923, and New York, Harcourt, 1959.

OSGOOD, C. E., SUKI, G. J., and TANNENBAUM, P. H.: *The Measurement of Meaning*, Urbana, Univ. of Illinois Press, 1957.

QUIRK, R.: *The Use of English*, London, Longmans, 1961, and New York, St. Martin's Press, 1963.

ROBINS, R. H.: *General Linguistics: An Introductory Survey*, London, Longmans, 1964.

DE SAUSSURE, F.: *Courses in General Linguistics*, New York, Philosophical Library, 1959.

STRANG, B. M. H.: *Modern English Structure*, London, Edward Arnold, 1962, and New York, St. Martin's Press, 1963.

ULLMANN, S.: *Semantics: An Introduction to the Science of Meaning*, Oxford, Blackwell, 1962.

WHORF, B. L.: *Language, Thought and Reality*, ed. J. B. Carroll, Cambridge, Mass., Technology Press of Mass. Inst. of Technology, 1956.

WITTGENSTEIN, L.: *Tractatus Logico-Philosophicus*, London, Routledge and Kegan Paul, 1961, and New York, Humanities Press; *Philosophical Investigations*, Oxford, Blackwell, and New York, Macmillan, 1953.